OVERCOME AND BECOME

OVERCOME AND BECOME

PORTRAITS IN WORDS OF
FIVE HEROIC PUNJABI WOMEN

PREET INDER DHILLON

www.whitefalconpublishing.com

Overcome and Become
Preet Inder Dhillon

www.whitefalconpublishing.com

All rights reserved
First Edition, 2019
© Preet Inder Dhillon, 2019
Cover design © White Falcon Publishing, 2019

No part of this publication may be reproduced, or stored in a retrieval system, or transmitted in any form by means of electronic, mechanical, photocopying or otherwise, without prior written permission from the author.

The contents of this book have been timestamped on the Ethereum blockchain as a permanent proof of existence. Scan the QR code or visit the URL given on the back cover to verify the blockchain certification for this book.

Requests for permission should be addressed to preetdhillon@hotmail.co.uk

ISBN - 978-93-89530-34-6

Everything I am is because of your blessings
My Maternal Grandad

S. HARCHARAN SINGH BOLINA

ABOUT THE AUTHOR

Born on 19 April 1973, Preet rediscovered herself as she stepped into her thirties. For more than half a decade, her regular weekly column in 'The Hindustan Times' and later in 'The Times of India' was well received and highly appreciated. Her debut book titled 'Rags to Ragas and Beyond' brought her glory and also 'The Women Achiever Award Canada'. Preet is a proficient radio presenter as well and has been a part of All India Radio for many years. Her absorbing voice and meaningful script have been her forte. Currently, she hosts an evening time radio show on Canada's leading Asian radio station, Cina Radio 1650 AM. An alumnus of St. Joseph's Convent School, Jalandhar, Preet earned a BA (Honours) degree from Hans Raj Mahila Mahavidyala and received the Masters degree in English Literature from DAV, Jalandhar. Presently, she lives in the United Kingdom with her husband – Hartej and her two sons – Navsher and Harshaan.

CONTENTS

Acknowledgements ix
Foreword xi
From the Writer's Desk xv

☆ Safar-E-Zindagi of Malika-E-Sur
   Surinder Kaur 1

☆ Amrita Pritam – The Woman Who Dared........57

☆ Eh Janam Tumhare Lekhe
   Dr. Inderjit Kaur 105

☆ Dr. Kiran Bedi – The One Woman Army 153

☆ Humaari Amrita
   Amrita Shergil – The Frida Kahlo of India.....201

ACKNOWLEDGMENTS

I would not be who I am today without the unconditional love of my family. My maternal Grand Father – Late S. Harcharan Singh's boundless love for us – sisters, till date gives me comfort and confidence to face anyone and anything. Special thanks to my sisters, my parents-in-law, my parents, my husband and my children for being by my side through every step of this process. Thank you to the amazing women in my life who have kept my spirits uplifted. You know who you are and what you mean to me. In fact, there's no me without you all.

There is absolutely no way that I could have completed this book in this lifetime without this amazing human named – Dolly Guleria. She kept me buoyed by her unwavering faith in my vision for this book. My grateful thanks to Dr. Inderjit Kaur for her cooperation in researching and writing this volume. Thank you Imroz ji and Dr. Kiran Bedi for helping me bring this book to life. I owe a debt of gratitude to the lady, who isn't just an amazing artist but fundamentally a very kind and generous human being – Divya Dutta. Thank you from the core of my heart for penning the foreword of the book. It means the world to me...

FOREWORD

GRIT AND GRACE

It's not every day that you receive a random call from a total stranger and you not only get talking but also agree to write a foreword for her. I was at shoot when I received a very warm message from Preet. What instantly touched me was her honesty and straightforwardness. All the questions that would probably arise in my head, she had already answered in her next message – who she was, why she had messaged, what she wanted and most importantly, why she thought, in spite of chatting for the first time and not knowing much about her, I would probably agree to do the needful. I loved her confidence. Her faith in herself and of course, our Punjabi bond.

Preet has her roots in rural Punjab. Her parents are into agriculture. In her growing up years, Preet – the eldest of the six children, was deeply hurt whenever she heard her father being addressed as *'Bechara'* because he had five daughters who they thought were a liability. Her parents did not give in to any pressures and went out of the way to educate their daughters. Her only aim is to make her parents proud…proud of their daughter…proud of their faith in her.

Preet, paper and pen have been the best of friends from the last one decade. They have been together – be it her columns in 'The Hindustan Times' and 'The Times of India' or her first book 'Rags To Ragas... And Beyond'. She called me regarding her second book which was about the five very inspiring women of Punjab. As soon as she named them, I knew I was going to be a part of this book. I was all set to write my foreword for this charming Punjabi girl who was writing on my most favourite Punjabi women – those who were known for their Punjabiyat and yet broke the stereotypes and stood up for their beliefs. They carved a niche for themselves in spite of oppositions. They stood tall in the male-dominated society with their own distinct identities. Today when you utter their names, a sense of pride seeps into the heart, along with a sense of warmth. As I finished reading what Preet has to write about their phenomenal journeys, I just feel so nostalgic... I, in a surreal way feel, like one with them... truly inspired by their lives and their works. Reading Preet's beautiful words on these phenomenal women, I reminisce my own connect with them.

I remember I had gone to the Khuswant Singh Literature Fest in Kasauli for the launch of my own book, 'Me and Ma' and I had also recited Amrita Pritam's *Main tainu pher milangi*'. I was in tears, and so was the audience... while reading Amrita's words, I could feel the pain and the hope and the love, all put together so beautifully by her. The event ended with me auctioning a *dupatta* which had the most amazing women of Punjab on it. The collects were to go for the education of the girl child. I had the honour of wearing that *dupatta* which had the images of Amrita Pritam, Amrita Shergil, Surinder Kaur on it.

The day I first heard the song *madhaniyaan* I burst into tears…just like Preet's mom and all the Punjabi women, I am sure, who understand the depth of that song and how Surinder Kaur ji sang and immortalised it. I remember, I instantly went and hugged my mom tight…not ready to leave her *pallu*. I felt so close to Surinder Kaur ji that when Dolly Guleria, her lovely daughter, who also in Preet's words, is a reflection of her mother, approached me for a video for her song, '*Ambarsare de Papad*' I instantly agreed. That in many ways made me feel extremely close to both the mother and the daughter.

Amrita Pritam, I am totally in love with – so much so that it's a dream someday to portray her on screen. The intensity, the sensitivity, the romance, the layers within… all in one lovely petite woman. And like Preet, in many ways I've befriended her too and my heart often says "*Kithe kis tarah pata nai, par main tainu pher milangi…*"

The life of Amrita Shergil has always intrigued me. Her life was filled with passion and colour just like her canvasses. Beautiful and brilliant, she lived it on her own terms, scandalizing the staid society of her times with her unconventional ways. And like Preet again, my first introduction to Amrita Shergil was that big sign board saying 'Amrita Shergil Marg'.

I've had the good fortune of interacting with Dr. Kiran Bedi. In my childhood, her name would pop up in my parents' conversations. She was mentioned as the Iron Lady who stood against all odds and was fearless. I looked up to her. In my school elocution class, I remember having said, "I want to be like Kiran Bedi." I got the chance to interact with her at a UNICEF event and she was all warmth – a lethal combination of cordiality and power, which is so rare.

Last but not the least, Dr. Inderjit Kaur ji who has immersed herself into the service of humanity through the Pingalwara.

Five gritty and inspiring Punjabi women. I didn't want the book to end... I wanted to keep reading more and more about them. Well done Preet! Each word you have penned has come straight from your heart and it's reached where it should, right into the hearts of the readers. Trust me, your parents will be so proud of you today and I pity the *Becharas* who called your father so.

I also feel that this book 'Overcome and Become' is not just about these five amazing women of Punjab. It's about each and every Punjabi girl who has dreams to pursue. It's a celebration of womanhood. The story of inspiration, the story of every female that includes – Surinder Kaur, Amrita Pritam, Dr. Kiran Bedi, Dr. Inderjit Kaur, Amrita Shergil, YOU, me and all the daughters of Punjab who are raring to fly.

In a surreal way again, Preet, I feel you have wrapped all the women of Punjab in that beautiful *dupatta* I wore...

Divya Dutta

FROM THE
WRITER'S DESK

My life started no differently than any other Punjabi girl. As far as I can recall, my gender has been a part of every discussion. My youngest sister, the fifth daughter of my parents, was born the year I, their firstborn, turned 11. I can precisely recollect my words when my *Naani maa* informed me about the new arrival in the family. "Can't we quietly throw her in the bin? Can't we leave her at the hospital? Why do we have to bring her home? My mummy already has four daughters. Everyone is yet again going to visit my daddy saying *ki koi naa sabr kar... Bechaare da ghar kuriyaan naal bharr gaya...*" Sounds awful! Doesn't it? A young 11-year-old child voicing such terrible words for her newborn sister. But trust me, they weren't my words. They were the words I had repeatedly heard over the years. They were the words my hypocritical society had drilled in my heart and mind ever since I gained consciousness. The society, I guess is clueless as to how it injures and scars the spirit and psyche of its daughters by continuously calling them a liability and their parents '*Bechare*' for having them.

This aversion for society's rules and norms is probably the reason that like a magnet, any gritty and brave woman to date pulls me towards her. I think in my formative years, I needed one brave hand to firmly hold mine...one confident voice to comfort me that I wasn't alone and that there were innumerable drops of water which with their perseverance had turned to fire... "*Before the fire, I too was water just like you...quenching the thirst of every dying creature... I gave and I gave until I turned into a desert from a sea... But instead of dying of heat, of sadness, and of tiredness, I gathered all my pain and all the tags the society had bestowed upon me, and from my own ashes I became fire.*"

Right from my school days, I kept looking for role models around me – in my home, in books. In my teens, when I was unsure and lacked confidence, I truly wished that an inspiring tale of a determined woman would take me in her arms and gently whisper in my ear, "If I can do it, so can you." But no story embraced me and I stumbled and got up yet again, alone. Hence the idea of writing such a book which would highlight the ups and downs, the highs and lows, the struggles and achievements of inspiring women personalities of Punjab was conceived way back, in my teens.

The most distinctive feature of the book 'Overcome and Become' is that although it is penned in English, yet it's Punjabi from head to toe. The *Punj* (five) protagonists of the book are the jewels that adorn my state – the Nightingale of Punjab – Surinder Kaur, the voice of every Punjabi girl – Amrita Pritam, the embodiment of humanity – Dr. Inderjit Kaur, the woman who dared – Dr. Kiran Bedi, and last but not the least – the woman who is an eloquent fusion between the east and the west – Amrita Shergil. The foreword of the book is yet again by another Punjabi inspiration, an artist par excellence – Divya Dutta. She isn't just a national award-winning actress, she's way beyond that – a compassionate, down to earth human and an ideal daughter who was, is and always shall be madly in love with her mother. Divya Dutta, in my eyes, is the best definition of an empowered Punjabi woman and I could see no one beyond her for penning the foreword of the book. The publisher of the book, another Punjabi woman entrepreneur – Navsangeet Kaur is the cherry on top. In a nutshell, 'Overcome and Become' is about the Punjabis, by a Punjabi, foreword by a Punjabi and published by yet another Punjabi woman.

When I picked my pen to begin with this book, my vision was to talk about the greatness, strength and commitment of these five women who have been my role models – not as a monolith but as a structure that is made up of many tiny interesting parts. I was curious about the things these inspiring women saw, heard, read or liked – because all of it determines why they think in a certain way. I have tried to absorb all I could about them and their lives. But given the limitations, I think the book is richer the way it grew organically, slowly. I cannot appreciate enough the many sources I used, including the various books, the many essays out there, the interviews on Youtube and in the newspapers. I greedily wanted to put in every detail that excited me and left me awestruck. Later I edited a lot, rather ruthlessly.

I wish the young readers would take a sense of wonder from the book. Firstly, to how incredibly magical, messy, and complex life is and secondly, I wish each reader would feel a sense of how seriously these women took their work and their missions. When girls, in particular, will read about women who went all out for what they believed in, they'll feel it is possible for them too. After reading the magical tales of their (S)Heroes, instead of a faraway dream, I am very sure, their aspirations will become real, concrete and achievable and womanhood would start to look more inviting because it's time to build queendoms out of wreckages and navigate through the chaos with nothing but the certainty of our inner voices.

So here's to all of the Queens and the Princesses –

Here's to all the strong women out there!
    Who stand up for themselves and face the world with a heart of a soldier.
    Here's to all the passionate women out there!
    Who won't let the world stop them from achieving their dreams and doing the things they love.
    Here's to all the independent women out there!
    Who have been there for themselves and show that they can.

Here's to all the unbreakable women out there!

Who have been knocked down countless times but they find a way to rise and stand up again.

Here's to all the women in this world

You are beautiful, you are worthy, and no one has the power to dim your light.

Preet Inder Dhillon

SAFAR-E-ZINDAGI OF MALIKA-E-SUR

SURINDER KAUR

JUNE 1985

It was a clear night as far as I can reminisce. The breeze blew warm announcing the coming of summer's hottest time. The aroma of the grass around was like an intoxicating perfume, and the starry night above was a painting more sublime than any man could create. Our entire family had spread out our '*Manje*' on the sprawling '*Vehra*' of our farmhouse. Lying there, I remember, counting the brightly shining stars and slipping into blissful sleep. Just as my eyelids were wilting, I heard my mum sobbing. I hastily got up, put my arms around her and asked, "What's the matter Maa? Are you okay?" As much as my maa tried to hold it in, the pain came out like an uproar from her throat in the form of a silent scream. The beads of salty water started falling down from her eyes, one after another. "Maa, you were okay a few minutes back. What happened all of a sudden?" I astoundingly questioned her. She looked towards me, kissed me on my forehead and said, "Surinder Kaur was singing 'Madhaaniyaan' on radio. Her voice took me along somewhere. And guess what! I saw you there, decked up as a beautiful bride. You were about to leave your maa's home behind." Once again, tears flowed unchecked down her cheeks and dripped from her chin. I was bewildered and couldn't fully comprehend as to what exactly Maa meant by all that. But today, I can relate to that feeling and it's not just me, Surinder Kaur's hypnotic voice interlaces every Punjabi mother-daughter duo in a single thread.

27 May 2019
Outside the school premises, Doncaster, England

I was there to pick up my daughter Nehmat from school. A year ten student, I spotted her walking towards the car, exhausted with dishevelled hair and conspicuously absent school tie. As I watched my daughter walk towards me, coincidentally came up a track in Surinder Kaur's enthralling voice on BBC Asian Radio Network, "*Maavan te dheeyan ral baithiyaa ni maaye koi kerdiyaa galoriyaan.*" I began envisioning Nehmat walking down the aisle to her future husband. A single tear slid down from my eyes, followed by another, yet another until a steady stream of salty tears flowed mellowing the sadness that engulfed me as I heard the song in Surinder Kaur's clear euphoric voice. I wondered where the difference between my mum's generation and mine was. Nothing, nothing at all… Feelings remain the same and so does the unconditional love between a mother and a daughter, and also the catalyst voice which multiplies their emotions and affection, till date, remains the same – Surinder Kaur's voice. My mother loved Surinder jee's voice. As I heard her absorbing voice, I hungered for more of her and my daughter relishes her songs too. Surinder Kaur's voice and songs have entwined so many generations in a single cord. There have been singers before her and plentiful after her as well but there isn't a single name that has left such profound impact on our essence, soul, spirit and culture. She could do justice to the words she enunciated because she lived each word, each relation of hers. We know her as 'The Nightingale of Punjab', but along with it, I see her as 'The Mother of Punjab and Punjabi Culture'.

Surinder Kaur's voice was actually my gateway to my mother tongue. Every Punjabi word she intoned in her crystal clear voice, in its sheer enunciation, surrendered its meaning so effortlessly. I started relishing her songs as I stepped into my teens. She sang so flawlessly, with no hiss or crackle, no dead moments…just flowing and encircling, transporting me to the place I hadn't ever been before. For me, Surinder Kaur was 'SUR-INDRA'/'The God of *Swar*' with an invisible halo around her head. Never even in the wildest of my dreams could I ever imagine then that one day I would get this 'once in a lifetime opportunity' to write about her voyage into the sonorous kingdom of music. My only regret though was that I missed meeting her, sitting by her side, hearing her talk about her journey, her sentiments, her passions. But the One up there, undeniably has His own way to answer any and every request you put forward. I met Dolly Guleria, Surinder Kaur's reflection, her daughter. After meeting Dolly, I felt 'The Mother of Punjabi Music' though was physically absent yet couldn't have been more present too. Surinder Kaur is everywhere – in her daughter's eyes, words, body, soul...literally all over the place. Dolly Guleria is her mother's mirror image. She wept counter-transferentially and her tears were the evidence of the fact, "Surinder Kaur hasn't left us. She lives in her daughter's soul and body."

But was Surinder Kaur's musical journey an easy one? What is it that makes certain entities keep at it? How does one adhere to the rigid, traditional framework and yet defy convention to emerge victorious? Probably, it's the grit to manage convictions in an exemplary way. What accounts for that iron will that refuses to take a bow, even when all the chips are down, and one may have reached the end of the road? It could be owing to that sterling ability to never say die and face life head-on. Or it could be when two souls became one, a bond that would help them grow – together! Her story certainly resonates and as soon as I scratched the surface it quickly became clear – "Like any other Punjabi woman's, her journey too wasn't a bed of roses." But Surinder Kaur being a woman of substance, she encountered all the debacles gracefully and remained calm, composed and courageous. Again, these three words bear testimony to her life, as she held on to this intrinsic belief:

> *NO SUCCESS IS FINAL,*
> *NO SORROW FATAL,*
> *IT'S THE COURAGE THAT COUNTS...*

And this bonding with her belief is what made her stand tall and apart from the rest...

2. ONCE UPON A TIME

Surinder Kaur, truly a roving cultural ambassador of Punjab, whose acclaim for her performances stemmed from the rigorous training she had under distinguished gurus right from the early years of her life. But how did this girl from the conservative, middle class Rajput Sikh family get to learn music and actually sing on the radio too? For those were the times when this art was restricted to professional singers or women of 'ill fame'. When she was growing up, girls from reputable and decent families did not sing except at family weddings or functions at home (and that too before an all-women audience). The only other singing allowed to girls was from Gurbani. In fact, the only music Surinder grew up with were the Punjabi folk songs sung at weddings, festivals and other functions in the heartland of 'Maajha' in what was the then central Punjab. Surinder's mother, Maya Devi, would often sing folk songs at home. So coherently, the first lessons in music came from her. Her elder sister, Prakash Kaur (who was eleven years older to her) exhibited a talent for singing and wished to learn music. Their father, Diwan Bishan Dass was a six feet two, sturdy, burly, progressive and highly literate being who worked as an assistant professor of chemistry at Government College, Lahore. Even though he was very broad-minded yet he did not approve of the idea of his daughter Prakash desiring to learn music professionally.

As destined, Surinder Kaur was born to sing. And when her *bhua* Kesaro (her father's sister) found that her Shindaan (She lovingly addressed Surinder by that name) was ardently inclined, even she backed her up with an obsessive zeal as if she was living her life via her *Shindaan*. Never did it occur to Surinder then, that one fine day her *bhua's* wisdom and discipline absorbed by her would become great assets in her career.

There's a Punjabi *Boli* (a short verse sung to the Gidha dance) which states, "*Nachan Wale Di Addi Naa Rehndi, Gaun wale da bol…*/the heel of a dancer and lips of a singer won't rest). So was it with these two euphonious sisters. Their voices just couldn't be silenced even as relatives tittle-tattled. To their good fortune, Surinder's elder brother, Harbans Singh (an officer in police) soon realised that his sisters had a veritable treasure. He took a stand saying, "If my Prakash *bheinji* is so passionate about music, she should be permitted to learn," thus opening the colossal iron gates of the sonorous kingdom of music for his sisters. In the later years, Prakash and Surinder had a rigorous Hindustani classical musical training under

Master Inayat Hussain, nephew of Bade Ghulam Ali Sahab and Niaz Hussain Shami from Sham Churasi Gharana. What a great experience it must have been for the girls being taught by such maestros at such a young age! They were so knowledgeable, so classical and when they sang, they simply enthralled. I can well imagine what privilege it would have been to sit down and learn from them. No other popular contemporary Punjabi singer except Nusrat Fateh Ali Khan Sahab has mastered the nuances of the Indian musical scale to the same extent.

The beginning wasn't an easy one for the girls. The neighbourhood was scandalised that the daughters of 'Sardars' were into singing. So for their 'Riyaaz' the girls would shut the doors, windows and even the ventilators lest the sound of music travelled outside. Prakash had an enchanting voice, and a natural twist in her voice made singing easy even for challenging classical notes. Lahore was the cradle of Punjabi culture then. It was home to a large number of folk songs and tunes. Prakash had mastered a lot of them from older ladies of her locality. She was a popular invitee to every wedding or engagement ceremony within her extended family. She used to take Surinder and even Narinder Kaur to accompany her to the gatherings. It was then that the two learnt to sing in unison and people simply loved it. Soon even strangers started inviting them and were actually willing to pay them which was a rarity during those days. So, whenever and wherever the two melodious sisters, Prakash and

Surinder sang, multitudes flocked to hear them and nobody ever went away unsatisfied. They constantly received ovations which showed the power of the witchery of their voices.

Although the postern, leading to this enormous unfathomable world of music, was unbolted by their brother, yet the path was new-fangled and definitely not an easy one because those were the days of Shamshad Begum and Zeenat Begum, both great singers in their own right and both coming from families of professional singers, and thus, singing wasn't a taboo for them. Prakash Kaur was the first 'Kaur' to break the shackles and taboos of her community to become the first radio singer in the family. Soon after, younger sister Surinder followed her. On 31 August 1943, Surinder went for auditions as an artist for the children's programmes but she was chosen for the adults section as a contractual artist at A.I.R Lahore by Jeevan Lal Mattoo (who headed the music section of AIR Lahore in 1940 as the producer and before that he was the program executive). Pandit Jeevan Lal himself was a great exponent of Kirana Gharana and had profound knowledge of Punjabi folk music and the Raaga Shastra. Young Surinder had no training in classical music yet Jeevan Lal selected her regardless of this drawback. He was well aware of the fact that even Amritsar-born Shamshad Begum, without any formal classical training, had become an accomplished singer and he saw the same potential in Surinder too. She learnt many things from Pandit Jeevan Lal who gave her some valued tips during auditions, and during her early singing career that helped her in improving her style.

Soon after auditions, Master Inayat Hussain, a freelance music director, invited Prakash and Surinder to sing a couple of songs under his direction. After repeated rehearsals, the sisters sang professionally in harmony. The first songs were, *"Haaye Naa Wass, Oye Naa Wass Badla, Aje Naa Wass Oye Kaaliya"* and *"Dhol Sipaahiya Vey Kithe Gayon Dil Laa Ke."* Both these songs became instant hits.

By 1944, one of the most prominent music composers from Lahore – Ghulam Haider had shifted to Bombay. Pandit Amarnath remained the reigning music director behind and his favourite singer undeniably was Zeenat Begum. Whatever Pandit Amarnath composed for Zeenat, young Surinder tried to copy it and sang it ceaselessly. Such was her keenness, allegiance and grit right from the early days.

Soon thereafter, Master Inayat Hussain composed another soul-stirring tune for Prakash and Surinder to sing as a duet – a song to be sung when the bride is about to leave her parents' house to make a home with her husband and his family. The song captures the tense and intense moments when the mother and daughter sit together for a while before the final parting. It goes thus, *"Maavaan Te Dheeyan Rall Baithiyaan Nee Maaye, Koi Kerdiyaa Galoriyaan, Kankaan Lamiyaan Dheeyan Kyo Jammiyaan Nee Maaye."* The sisters had heard their mother sing this song in long plaintive tone but for their recording, they gave a livelier beat while retaining its intensity.

This song was recorded in two parts, which was featured in two sides of the same disc. This record sold like hotcakes throughout Punjab and was on the lips of every Punjabi woman of that time and retains its popularity till date. Zeenat and Shamshad Begum had shifted to Bombay by then and the vacuum created in Lahore by their move was filled up by the two sisters – Prakash and Surinder.

Budh Singh Taan was another versatile virtuoso who could shift roles between a music director and a radio singer. Bhai Santa Singh and Bhai Samund Singh were the leading Sikh religious musicians and Budh Singh Taan was the third such musician at All India Radio, Lahore. He is credited with the recording of the first-ever complete 'Aasa Di Waar'. Budh Singh Taan did not record it in Lahore's own 'Jeno Phone studio', which had its own music director and orchestra, but went to Bombay to record it in the studios of newly opened 'Young India Recording Company' in Wadala, Bombay. Budh Singh Taan composed two tunes of *Shabads* for Surinder Kaur to sing. One of them was Guru Nanak's *Shabad*, "*Vaid Bulaaya Vaidgy, Meri Pakar Dhandole Baanh.*" This record also sold extremely well in Lahore and Amritsar. Surinder Kaur was by now basking in the glory of her well-recognised talent and she seemed to enjoy every tiny bit of it. They had hired a harmonium player and a dholki player to accompany them at all the pre-wedding musical gigs.

3. THIS SIDE, THAT SIDE – PANGS OF PARTITION

Isi sarhad pe kal dooba tha sooraj ho ke do tukade,
isi sarhad pe kal zakhmi huyi thi subh-e-azaadi...

Surinder's world was just so picture-perfect and seamless in those days. But the harsh reality is that life is unpredictable and the belief that we control it, is merely an illusion. Sometimes all this whimsicality becomes overwhelming and makes us feel small and powerless. And that's exactly what happened during the partition phase. By 1945, people in the streets were talking about the creation of Pakistan, and Lahore being a part of it. Surinder was a naïve young girl who never thought anything unfortunate could happen to the city she so dearly loved. She got the scare of her life when she heard that in March 1947 many innocent Sikhs were burnt at a Gurudwara in Rawalpindi district. This disastrous news created tension in Lahore too because the city had more of the Hindu and Sikh population. There were speculations as to which nation would get Lahore. A large section of the press was pleading for Lahore's inclusion in India. Pakistan became independent first and Lahore was included in it on 14 August 1947. Overnight All India Radio Lahore became Radio Pakistan Lahore and the tone of the radio and pro-Pakistan newspapers changed.

Surinder's world which had been stable for many years collapsed in just one night. That particular night, one 'Mohalla' of Lahore inhabited entirely by the Hindus was set ablaze. Some people perished in the inferno, others left in a jiffy. A lot of Sikhs were killed in gun battles and in attacks with sharp weapons. Their homes were blown away in the ferocious winds of human rage gusting along the border. Loaded, affluent people turned paupers overnight. A hastily-drawn Radcliffe Line saw a single nation bifurcated, and later trifurcated into three different entities. It left millions confused about their identity as they were compelled to set up home in another part of the subcontinent, rootless and penniless, and struck numb by the loss of near and dear ones to cruel marauders who were themselves victims to religious brainwashing and propaganda. The land that had been home to generations became foreign land. It was beyond belief that fencing and borders would prevent them from ever going back to where they had belonged. Everything familiar was snatched off cruelly overnight; leaving confusion and the loss of identity in its wake.

Nevertheless, Surinder's family was determined to make a new beginning. They decided not to go to

Amritsar, which was the nearest city, but to a more imperturbable city – Ferozepur. The family, without much to carry along, joined a 'Qaafila' to Kasur and Ferozepur. The caravan progressed sluggishly. On both sides, there was stench of death. Few more joined them on the way and shared stories of cruelty and wanton destruction. No one was spared – not even the old or the infants. The stories emerging out of Gujranwala, Sheikhupura and Nankana Sahib were the most heartrending. Somehow Surinder with family crossed Kasur and approached Ganda Singhwala. On reaching Ganda Singhwala, they heaved a sigh of relief. Ferozepur was only fifteen kilometres from there. There were hordes of burly Sikhs moving towards Ferozepur. Surinder's family joined them too. A few steps from Hussainiwala was the Indian border. As soon as they touched the Indian Territory, smiles returned to their comatose faces. Although they saw many grim faces of the Muslims heading to Pakistan. What madness was it!

As I am trying to pick the shells of aches and pangs of partition as I stroll at the shores of Surinder Kaur's life, get hazy in her experiences and allow the salt of her memories to cling to my hands and feet, I am reminded of a reflective verse penned by Nida Fazli...

Insaan Mien Haiwaan, Yahaan Bhi hai, Wahaan Bhi,
Alaah Nigebaan, Yahaan bhi Hai, Wahaan Bhi...
Rehmaan Ki Kudrat Ho Yaa Bhagwaan Ki Moorat,
Her Kheil Kaa Maidaan, Yahaan Bhi hai Wahaan Bhi...
Hindu Bhi Mazey mein Hain, Musalmaan Bhi Mazey Mein,
Insaan Pareshaan Yahaan Bhi hai, Wahaan Bhi...

On reaching Ferozepur, Surinder discovered that life was far better in Lahore. They were much less in demand in Ferozepur and at times they had to sleep without food. As September approached, they learnt that in Pakistan, the violence had subsided, but in Amritsar, the frenzy was on the increase. Although in the beginning of August, East Punjab had been peaceful, but after the 15th of August, when trainloads of dead had arrived at Amritsar's Main Railway Station, people in the villages got out of control. Even the government could not calm them. Ferozepur was relatively peaceful. Surinder Kaur stayed for a few months in Ferozepur before moving to Ghaziabad with her parents.

4. HAPPILY EVER AFTER

Nearly a year back, I saw a very inspiring Bollywood film with Priyanka Chopra in the lead role playing the role of real-life 'Mary Kom'. The movie certainly presents an exemplary effort on the part of its cast and crew, to showcase a talented sportsperson who has done her country immensely proud. Back then while everyone was celebrating and talking about Mary Kom's victories, courage and grit (which I did as well) I felt the film is way beyond attainments and triumphs. I take it as 'the most beautiful tale of love, companionship and living each other's dreams as a couple'. Undeniably, the world would have forgotten 'Mary' long time back, had there been no 'Onler' in her life. At times I really wonder, "Why men like Onler are such rare species of mankind? Do husbands like him really exist in today's world?" Currently, as I am reading, researching, skimming and scanning through the pages of our melodic treasure – Surinder Kaur's life, many of my subjective qualms (as a woman) are being countered/replied back. 'Behind every successful man, there's a woman' goes the conventional adage but after scrutinizing the archives of Surinder Kaur's life, with faith, pride and conviction I give away the crux of her life – *Behind this great woman Surinder Kaur, was an even greater man, her husband – S. Joginder Singh Sodhi.*

And this is how the fairy tale began... I guess it must have been ordained that one fortunate day, Surinder Kaur (born on 25 November 1929) was to meet S. Joginder Singh Sodhi (born on 18 January 1923) in Lahore at her brother's house. Joginder's cousin, Jagdish Kaur, was married to Surinder's brother, Jaswant Singh. Both their families desired for their union but the question was who would bell the cat? Because had Surinder known about the intents of her family, she wouldn't have agreed to visit her brother along with her father that day. Finally, 'Jab They Met', the very same evening they got hooked up and after that their 'arranged love story' just unfolded naturally. After the first meeting, the verdict by the seniors of both the families was, "*Jhat Pat Mangni Da Intezaam Karo.*" Soon after, they were engaged. All that happened during the initial months of 1947. The nation at that time was already going through extreme agony and misery. And then, the Partition happened – "*Pher, koi kittey te koi kittey.*"

Joginder Singh moved to Preet Nagar and began serving as an educationalist at S. Gurbaksh Singh

Preetlari's school. As luck be, many of his friends from Lahore joined him there. Dr. Inderjit Singh, Achla Sachdeva, Gyaan Sachdeva, Balwant Gargi, Prem Sachdeva, Taara Singh Chann, Preet Maan, Navtej Singh (the eldest son of S. Gurbaksh Singh) – all of them started envisaging a new India, a free India. They all desired to contribute in their own way in sprinkling awareness in general public through plays and inspirational lyrics and songs. That was the time when Joginder's friends would tease him saying, *"Kithe gayi teri bulbul? Aainvai khwaab hi dekhda rehnda aain yaa haqeeqat vi banegi?"*

It was 29 January 1948 – the day Surinder Kaur and Joginder Singh got married; they merged into each other irrevocably and rather from that day onwards, their two entwined souls started going and flowing the same way, in the same direction. Just a handful of guests – five, to be more precise (the groom himself, Dr. Inderjit Singh, Gyaan Sachdeva, Balwant Gargi and Bhupinder Singh) went to Sahibabad for a very small, intimate and streamlined wedding ceremony. The *Doli* went straight to Balwant Gargi's residence (1/2 Curzon Road, New Delhi). It had already been planned that the newly married couple would move to Bombay in the days to come. Joginder Singh often recounted an episode – while on their way to Bombay as the train rustled through lush green meadows, Joginder transformed his feelings into words, beheld his newly wedded bride and murmured, "Our new life together is going to be as serene and strikingly beautiful as these leas and grasslands." Upon hearing these words, 18-year-old Surinder started laughing incessantly and innocuously questioned, "Are we going to live in the fields from now on?" That was the moment when Joginder Singh realised that he had married a very childlike, ingenuous, naïve lass who wasn't even conscious of the invincible talent she was blessed with. Right from that moment, he made it an integral aim of his life to navigate his wife's genius into unprecedented greatness.

After reaching Bombay, Joginder Singh started working as an assistant director with his friend – Ramesh Sehgal. It was then that Surinder Kaur got an opportunity to meet various distinguished music directors. Henceforth began a new inning of her life. Instantaneously recordings began with Hussan Lal, Bhagat Ram, Shri Ram Chandra, Ghulam Haider, Sardool Kawatra, S. Mohinder, Begum Akhtar, Pt. Ravi Shankar, Vyas Rao Pat Vardan and Hans Raj Behal.

Incidentally, S. Mukherjee refused to let the newcomer Lata Mangeshkar do the playback in *Shaheed* for Kamini Kaushal saying that her voice was too thin and shrill. Ghulam Haider summoned Surinder Kaur to sing '*Badnaam na ho jaye mohabat ka fasana, Ujda umeedon ka chaman ab hum kahan aur tum kahan, Aana hai to aa jao gar ab bhee na aaogey hum tumko na payengey tum humko na paogey*'. The popularity of *Shaheed* numbers took Surinder Kaur to dizzy heights and she overshadowed Zohrabai Ambalawali, Ameerbai Karnataki, Raj Kumari, Noor Jahan, Shamshaad Begum, etc. who ruled the roost at that time. Her scintillating and tantalising voice struck a chord with music lovers when she sang '*Ab jiyen batao kis ke liye*' and '*Akhiyan milake ankhiyan roen din ratiyan*' in films *Sanwariya* and *Nadiya Ke Paar* under the baton of maestro C. Ramchandra.

Her duets '*Keh do hamen na beqrar kare who jise mera dil pyar karey*' with Mohammed Rafi, '*Tera kisi se pyar thha ab woh zamana bhool ja*' with Mukesh and '*Haye chan vey ki khatya ae dil la ke*' with Talat Mahmood in films *Sabak*, *Dada* and Punjabi film *Mutiyar* respectively bring a nostalgic lump to the throat even today.

Surinder Kaur was luxuriating her celebrity eminence and had even bought a sea-facing, well-appointed flat in Bombay's posh colony but all that didn't last for too long. Severe appendicitis pain exhausted her emotionally and physically. All she desired was to go back to her parents at Ghaziabad. Dr. Puri operated on her at Narendra place, Delhi, and within a few days Surinder was hale and hearty but she never agreed to move back to Bombay again.

As soon as she recuperated from her illness in 1953, she began singing first from Jalandhar Radio and then from Delhi Radio. The same year major British record label – HMV approached Surinder and signed her as their artist. From there on, there has been no looking back for her…each melody of hers, till date, pierces through the souls of her listeners like a sharp dagger.

After their eventful move to New Delhi, S. Joginder Singh Sodhi took a professorial job. After finishing his daily academic responsibilities during and after college hours, Professor Sodhi would start going through the recent poetry of the all-time great poets and lyricists of Punjabi language. He did not want Surinder to sing any substandard song and for that Masters in psychology wasn't enough. Hence he enrolled himself for masters in Punjabi literature at Delhi University. He would meticulously go through the works of Amrita Pritam, the folk poet Nand Lal Nurpuri, Dhani Ram Chatrik, Professor Mohan Singh, Shiv Kumar Batalvi, Bishan Singh Upashak and Parkash Saathi to name a few. Every few days, Joginder would identify a piece of poetry for Surinder to sing and record.

While Surinder was immensely busy, Professor Sodhi used to do the rounds of various music directors based in Delhi – e.g. K. Panna Lal, Kesar Singh Narula, Mujjaddid Niazi and Pandit Amar Nath (Junior) to name a few. He would discuss the chosen lyrics with the music director. The music director would come up with a suitable '*Taal*' and the '*Raag*'and would also compose a number of would-be tunes. One of those tunes used to become the common choice of Joginder and the music composer. Before Surinder arrived at the studios for rehearsals and eventual recordings, the compositions were already finalized and fine-tuned. Those were the golden days of Punjabi music and Surinder Kaur was crowned as 'The Queen of Punjabi Music'. Within a few years, she attained the status of being the Nightingale of Punjab.

Not merely at the work front, Joginder Singh, the primary caregiver to their three daughters, was the cornerstone of support for Surinder. Their eldest daughter, Dolly, reminiscences, "I must have been around three and a half years old, when Mama was selected by the then Prime Minister of India, Pandit Jawaharlal Nehru as the cultural ambassador of Punjab to be a part of the delegation to represent India in different nations. It was a team of highly proficient gifted artists including Nargis, Raj Kapoor, Balraj Sahni, Nirupa Roy and singer Aasa Singh Mastana. They were supposed to be touring various countries primarily China, Russia, Afghanistan as a part of the cultural exchange forum for around six months at a stretch. Mama was reluctant as she didn't want to leave her young child behind for so long. And then as usual, Mama's super hero and saviour (my father) Daarji stepped in to convince her and to take the baggage of guilt off her shoulders. Daarji joined the child guidance school at Karol Bagh as a teacher where he would take me along. For nearly six months he was my mother and father both. Daarji truly was the wind beneath mama's wings."

With so much of negativity, ego issues and chauvinism around, the tale of this *'made and lived for each other couple'* is like a whiff of fresh air. I feel like celebrating their life, singing at the top of my crude voice…(From Her to Him)

It must have been cold there in my shadow,
To never have sunlight on your face.
You were content to let me shine, that's your way.
You always walked a step behind.
So I was the one with all the glory,
While you were the one with all the strength.

A beautiful face without a name for so long.
A beautiful smile to hide the pain.
Did you ever know that you're my hero,
And everything I would like to be?
I can fly higher than an eagle,
For you are the wind beneath my wings.

5. MEHRAM DILAA DE MAAHI, MOREINGA KADD MUHAARAN

On 28 August 1976 at 9:45 in the morning, Surinder Kaur's world came crumbling down. Her friend, philosopher, mentor, guide, best wisher, redeemer, protector, her husband – Professor Joginder Singh Sodhi passed away. From the last six days, ever since her husband had been admitted to the hospital, her soul had been constantly on its knees, praying unendingly. She sobbed into her hands and the tears dripped between her fingers, raining down onto the parched earth. She had been literally pleading the doctors to save her husband. "How am I supposed to live without him?" hysterically she questioned everyone present there. She cried as if the ferocity of it would bring her husband back…as if by the sheer intensity of her tears, the news would be undone. She cried until no more tears came,

but still the emptiness and sorrow lingered. On the first light of the next day, Surinder's still crouched figure remained unmoved. There was nothing left; nobody left, no reason to move.

At the prayer ceremony held at Gurudwara Model Town on September 5, countless people came to pay their reverences to the "*Peer fakir jis ne apni mehbooba, shareeke hayaat – Surinder nu aasmaan diyaa bulandiyaa te pahunchaaya, sangeet di duniya vich us nu star banaaya.*" The innumerable bouquets placed before Joginder Singh's picture seemed like a mammoth ocean of blossoms. Memories came flooding back. Every now and then for the past many years, he would present a bouquet of yellow flowers to his wife and say, "Yellow rose of Texas, you are the only girl for me."

With each passing day, the reality of the colossal loss shadowed Surinder. She could feel that the threads of each memory of her husband had tied up her hands and feet. Her knees dug into the earth, her hands unsteady as they silently clawed at the clay. She tried to open her mouth, but not a sound came out. Surinder's eyes went blank as if they had lost all sight. Her mouth opened, an eternal silenced scream, stained with the memory of the man she so dearly loved and worshipped. He was an angel, always shielding her from the glare of the outside world.

The days that followed Joginder Singh's death were completely empty. Most of the time Surinder sleep-walked through the things she had to do, so numb that she wasn't even completely aware as to what was happening around her, cut off from everything that she thought was her life. It seemed as if she was standing on an unfamiliar shore, confused and lost. At the young age of 46, her husband's demise had left her traumatised and shattered. Joginder Singh stole a bit of Surinder and carried a few pieces of her along with him to the spirit world – her smiles, her confidence and her zeal to live. She wasn't the same person anymore and for some time, everyone thought that she wouldn't ever sing again.

A few months later, an annual conference of Delhi Radio was to be held and Mr. Satish Bhatia, who was the chief composer of All India Radio, Delhi, implored Surinder Kaur to participate at the event. He was so obdurate that he wouldn't take no for an answer. After the event, the following day all the major newspapers carried the same headlines, 'Surinder Kaur sang the way she never has till date, breaking her own record of melodious singing'. In that gathering, she sang Shiv Kumar Batalvi's composition, '*Vaasta eh mera mere dilaa deyaa mehramaa, fuliyaa kaneraan ghar aa jaa*'. She sobbed as she sang and the audience was in tears too.

With time, at All India Radio, Surinder started singing sad Urdu Ghazals composed by all-time greats like Mirza Ghalib. Since these were the renditions coming from her heart and soul, they had a tremendous impact on the audiences. Some of the Punjabi Ghazals recorded in her voice have attained the status of evergreen pieces of music. Some of these such as '*Vichhrhe chiran ton uh mainoo supne che mil gaye, aya unhan daa naa mere athroo nikal gaye'*, *'Inhan akhiyan che pawan kivenye kajla veh akhiyan che toon vasda'*, *'Mehram dilan de maahi, morhen ga kad muharan, din raat ne arman kayi hazaran'* and *'Oh barha belihaaz ki kariye, bewafa da illaj ki kariye'* are still very fresh in the memories of listeners. These recordings in her voice are her most emotionally rendered numbers.

The gate outside Surinder Kaur's home still bears a nameplate with two names – Joginder Singh and Surinder Kaur. "I moved to this house from Model Town after his death. Let me tell you something. My favourite flower is the rose. We had a generous number of roses in our garden at our Model Town residence. But after his death, roses just did not bloom in my garden. I kept the nameplate as it was. It pained me to remove his name. During the killings of the Sikhs in November 1984, my neighbours got worried about me. They asked me to take off the nameplate. But I refused. If death has to come, I'll welcome her. But they took off the nameplate without informing me, out of concern. When normalcy returned, I put the nameplate right back," she shared (excerpt from a television interview of Surinder Kaur recorded in the nineties).

Losing the strong emotional anchor Surinder had in her husband, she went through depression for a few years. Her daughter Dolly recalls, "For a while, Mama was very pessimistic and despondent. She felt so bereft, so diminished as if the very foundation of her existence had been shaken. For a long time, she was totally clueless and her life was in shambles. But then it was our turn to aid her emotionally. Moreover, *Gurbani* helped her come to terms with her colossal loss. In addition to this, mama's admirers who continued to yearn for her songs helped her come out of this rut."

As everyone says 'time is the best healer', the shattered wife in Surinder Kaur took a back seat and the mother in her gathered all her fragmented bits of courage to look after her three daughters – Rupini (Dolly), Nandini (Nandi) and Promodini (Baby).

Dolly remembers an incident vividly when she annoyingly told her mother Surinder one evening, "Mama, you love Nandi more than me. You aren't bothered a bit about my happiness. I have always been only my Daarji's daughter and now that he has left, I have nobody in the world to love and protect me." Surinder hugged her daughter securely and cried as if the child within her had been pricked in through the protective layers of maturity. She whispered, "*Meriye bachiye... Eh gal murr ke kadi nai kehni jadd tak mein zinda haan.*"

Dolly and her sisters as a ritual used to tie *rakhi* on their father's wrist till he was physically with them (probably their Daarji did not want them to feel the void of not having a brother) but after that incident, Surinder Kaur made sure that her daughters tied her *rakhi* instead. For the sake of her daughters, she became a fighter who battled with the fear inside her because she knew that without her the lives of her daughters would dissolve into chaos. Undeniably, the strength of motherhood proved greater than the natural laws.

Memories are immortal, we live with them till our last breath. Surinder Kaur wasn't an exception. Today, with both physically gone, as I am flipping through the pages of their lives, I am reminded of this poem, *Dark Eyes* that I read in school:

Life has been so long
But alone I mourn for you
Love of mine.
Is there ever a sign
On your paths to show
The way that I must go?
Gone the joys I knew
They all went with you.
What is left to me
MEMORY......

6. HER MEHMAAN NAWAAZI

My maternal granddad often used to say, "*Wadda insaan oh nai hunda, jis kol wadda ghar yaa waddi gaddi hoye, haan, oh zaroor hunda hai, jis kol waddi soch te wadda dil hoye.*" As I am passing through the slender, curvy path of life, experiencing its beauty and ugliness and trying to differentiate between real and superficial, I feel all the more indebted and appreciative of '*my nanaji's*' words and thoughts. What a proud and gratifying feeling it is to pen the life of the '*Waddi, uchi te suchi rooh – Surinder Kaur*'!

Surinder Kaur was an extremely self-effacing lady who was immensely fond of cooking and feeding others (at times forcibly). Dolly Guleria, her eldest daughter couldn't help smiling as she narrated an incident. "India's 7th President Gyani Zail Singh was mama's elder brother-in-law's (Sukhdev Singh Virdi – her sister's husband) uncle. Gyani ji along with Sukhdev uncle and an aged person from their village, came to visit mama. It was extremely cold outside and the chilly weather's harsh bites could be felt through the warm coats. After a brief chit chat, lunch was served. The aged uncle contentedly sat on the carpet with his plate, with the room heater right behind him.

Mama was repeatedly saying, '*Eh lao naa, oh lao naa, hor khao naa.*' All of a sudden, the room was submerged in a very strange odour as if something was burning. And it certainly was – that aged uncle's coat. He had moved too close to the room heater because every time mama said, '*Thora hor lai lao*' he slipped back slightly. When he realised it was his coat roasting, he instantly got up and furiously told mama, '*Khaana khwaeingi ke saareingi bibi meinu.*' Awkwardly, there wasn't any pretence of sympathy or mad rush to unscramble that aged uncle from his coat. Rather, a tittle rippled across the silent room which exploded into fits of laughter later. Mama apologised but couldn't resist asking, '*Tusi har waar piche kyo hoyi jande si?*' The aged person, with a shy grin which was overloaded with warmth, replied, '*Bibi, tu taan magar hi pai gayi si. Kina khaa sakda koi.*' I felt, the deep curve on Dolly's lips as she shared the incident about her mother's renowned '*mehmaan nawaazi*' was like a smile with a twist to it, like the smile of a child who is determined not to weep.

Surinder Kaur's home was a place where visitors loved to go again and again, and the evident reason was the exultant combination of the meals she prepared and the attention she showered. Surinder was a flawless hostess, her tagline being, "*Koi khatraa nai bacheya, hor lai lavo…thora horr…*"

Cooking was something she really enjoyed. To cook was to find her peace and her kitchen held the keys to serenity. "I love it the way when from all the chaos and raw ingredients emerges something beautiful," Surinder would often say. The jumble of flour and the salt garnished with love and care was her interpretation of hospitality. Renowned Punjabi language dramatist, theatre director, novelist and academic – Balwant Gargi made a documentary film on Surinder Kaur's life in which he explicitly revealed about '*her unique style of hospitality*'. He was impressively in love with Surinder's handmade *paranthas*. He often cited about the *vegetable pulao* that was served on Surinder's wedding day. What made that dish distinctive was the fact that even on her own wedding day, she prepared that *pulao* with her own hands dusting it with oodles of love, warmth and affection.

Every now and then, somebody would drop a melting in the mouth, rich and sweet *mithai box* at Surinder's home and she would be more than ecstatic holding the *mithai wala dabba* in her hands. For the coming few days, all the delights in one box were like sensory overload, a form of choice paralysis but after a short span, the pleasure vaporized and all the leftover *mithai* landed into a big container of boiling milk accompanied by lots of dry fruit and condensed milk. Dolly recollected, "Mama would keep looking for a prey to have that special dessert of hers. She wanted all her daughters to try her rich new invention but we all outspokenly denied being guinea pigs for mama's '*freshly made pudding from stale sweets*' and then she would start looking for new target. The search usually ended at one person – Sharanjit Singh Guleria, my husband, who couldn't ever say no to Mama.

She would normally say, '*Sharanjit, dass ehna kuriyaa nu mein kini swaadi pudding banai hai. Eh kuriyaa te badtameez hun, meri pakai nai khaandiyaa'*." As of today, Dolly is willing to barter infinite riches of the world for that handmade dessert by her mother. Alas! It's too late. "Mama's speciality was *suji da halwa* and I don't know how, but even today when I prepare it, my house smells of mama's cooking." Dolly's lower lip quivered as words slowly made their way out of her mouth while her eyes became glazed with a glassy layer of tears.

The festive spirit usually returned to Surinder's home as soon as she entered the gates of her place after stretched, exhausting tours and concerts. The dining table would be laden with delicacies. The rich aroma of *fried fish, sarson da saag, paneer, kabaabs, pudina chutney, karri pakore and some chatpata achaar* wafted down and beckoned her. These were all Surinder Kaur's favourite food items.

Expressing gratitude for the motherly love Surinder Kaur bequeathed on him, prominent Sufi singer, Hans Raj Hans recalled an unforgettable incident while Surinder Kaur was staying with her daughters Nandini and Parmodini at New Jersey, USA. Hans opined, "Surinder Kaur ji came to know that I was in America. She called and invited me over to her place for a Punjabi meal. It was a dark moonless night and the cold had stolen every bit of water from the air to frost over the countryside. In such a horribly cold weather, I found her standing outside her home, waiting for me. She wrapped me up in her warm motherly embrace and welcomed me. I can never forget the *sarson ka saag* she had especially cooked for me. Moreover, the way she repeatedly said '*Bacheya thora hor, bas thora jeha hor lai*' took me to my village Shaffipur when my mother would feed me with the same affection. That's why I always say ki '*Oh sirf apniyaa betiyaan di maa nai si, oh her ik Punjabi di maa si. Sab ton khoobsoorat rooh.*' After meal, we all sat together and I sang her a hit song *Mehram dilan de maahi* and she advised me to retain humility and uprightness, which would embellish my art."

As I am imprisoning in words the incredible shades of the amazing lady Surinder Kaur, I am forced to halt in between…I close my eyes letting my mind fill up with her voice and I wish…I wish I could bring her out of the photo frames… I wish I was fortunate enough to have met her…I sincerely wish…

7. BEYOND MUSIC

With the spread of conformity and image-driven superficiality, the allure of an individuated woman in full possession of herself and her powers, whatever we may say or however we may define beauty, is still irresistible. That's the reason that Surinder Kaur was somebody more than beautiful, something alchemical, a mixture of rare elements bound together by nerve and charm. She was simplicity and charm personified.

Surinder and her undying love for velvety clothes and her *suits* was an open secret. She would always be impeccably dressed up in a fine Punjabi suit, with a slim, slender chain around her neck, diamond studs and a gold bracelet with a *karra* from Shri Harmandir Sahib in each wrist of hers. One of her admirers once asked her as to why she was always so merely dressed, with no adornments to further embellish her beauty? Swiftly, beneath the two glowing eyes appeared a grin and she said, *"Tuhade saareyaa da pyar hi mera gehna hai. Kalaakaar di pehchaan us de chahaun waaleyaa ton bandi hai te oh hi us nu sajaunde hun."* Moreover Surinder was God's favourite child whom He already had bedizened with *'Sur da Gehna/The ornament of Sur'*, so there wasn't much need to prettify her neck with adornments when her throat already had been bejewelled.

The single thing Surinder was sensitive about was her *'dusky complexion'* and she would perpetually joke about it and say, *"Mein kaali haan, es layi meinu koyal da khitaab mileya hai."* Surinder would often instruct her makeup artist, *"Meinu thora gora bana devin."* In actuality, her hazy skin was completely flawless. I wonder if she used face masks or expensive skin care products. She was all about simplicity, making things easy, helping those around her relax and be happy with what they have. Perhaps, that is why her skin glowed and it was her inner beauty that lit her eyes and softened her features. When she smiled and laughed, you couldn't help but smile along too, even if it was just on the inside.

Dolly Guleria shared an interesting anecdote in this context, "Once a photographer gifted Mama a picture of hers which he had randomly clicked a long time back. Maa fell in love with that portrait of hers primarily because she felt she looked fair in that picture. Her smile was just like a warm embrace when she said, '*Veh tu meinu barra change lagnaa eh... tu te meinu tasveer vich gori mei'm hi bana dita eh*', to which the photographer replied, '*Maa, tu te meinu sadda hi gori lagdi hain.*' From that very moment, the photographer became my Mama's son. Actually, we all were well-aware of the fact that whichever country, city or place she visited, she eventually ended up making somebody her son. At times I thought that was 'coz Mama had three daughters of her own and probably she missed having a son (although that's merely an assumption) but gratefully the Almighty filled up that void by making her – *the Mother of Punjabi Music and of millions of Punjabis residing in India and abroad.*" I could see the proud daughter's orbs scintillating with a gratified glint as she spoke about her mother, the Empress of Melody – Surinder Kaur.

Surinder was one charismatic queen who wore many crowns. She was a fine amalgamation of talent and relations – the lady who lived and treasured all her relations as much as she cherished her singing. She was an affectionate daughter, a devoted wife, a gentle mother, a caring sister and above all, an extremely compassionate human being. She was the second youngest out of the ten siblings (they were five sisters and five brothers). Surinder's brother *Jaswant Singh* was the eldest, followed by her sisters *Prakash Kaur* and *Mahendra Kaur* and brothers – *Harbans Singh,*

Harbhajan Singh, Gurbachan Singh Senior. The next in the row was her sister *Manjit Kaur* and brother *Gurbachan Singh Junior*. *Surinder* was the ninth child in the family followed by her youngest sister *Narendra Pal*. All the siblings were like chalk and cheese yet they were each other's harbour and emotional morphine. Dolly has cited about the sensitive, profound bond between her mother and her siblings in her book, '*Wagde Paaniyaa da Sangeet*' which is a dedication for her parents – S. Joginder Singh and Surinder Kaur. In that volume, she shared, "Manjit Maasi was merely two years elder to Mama and they both shared a very emotional bond. Manjit Maasi and Narayan Singh Uncle (her husband) had no child of their own. Mama could feel the vacuum and their pain. Such an ache is different and more intense than the pain of a cut or bruise, and it stings with every breath one takes. This invisible scar on Maasi's psyche was something mama tried healing with the most gentle of her touch. Narayan Uncle passed away in 2001 and while on his deathbed, he told mama, '*Hun mera vela aaoun wala hai…Manjit da khyaal tu hi rakh sakdi ein, hor koi nai.*' Right from that moment, their roles reversed. Mama started caring for her elder sister like a newborn. She would feed Maasi before she had her own meals. She went to bed only after she put Maasi to sleep. Countless times she would get up in a single night to check if her sister was well and enjoying a sound sleep. Both of them had perfected a language of snarls and smiles, frowns and winks, sniffs and sorts and gasps and sigh! Mama and Manjit Maasi were like Siamese twins joined emotionally. Together they would enjoy music, watch television shows, pray, eat and gossip." After narrating the yarn, Dolly showed me pictures of her mother with her brothers and sisters. Those celluloid stills are conduits to her best memories till date and for a few minutes, I felt she was lost in the transitory evocation of her days with her mother, Surinder Kaur. Whatever we may say, it's ironical that the most beautiful memories are the worst ones too, cutting us from inside as if they are shards of glass.

Ravneet Guleria, Dolly's daughter-in-law, remembers her *Naani Maa/Naani Saas* – Surinder Kaur as the epitome of pious and unconditional love. "Arthritis had reduced Manjit Maasi's fingers to gnarled and painful twists of hardened skin and muscle while her bones crippled beyond repair. All through her last years, naani maa became her sister's angel and wonder woman who enthralled in a lucent guise, had the power to heal her pain. You should have seen the sisters in each other's company...it indeed was a slice of heaven. Naani Maa's aura was an elixir...unconditional love swam in her eyes for her sister. *'Eh koi ehsaan nai hai bacheya, mera farz hai....je mein nai karaangi te meri bhein da khyaal kaun rakhega'* she would often say. The world knows Naani Maa as the lady with a silvery, mellifluous voice but she was way beyond that. She was the most tranquil yet spirited person...someone who could ignite empathy within you...she was love, true love, pure love, everlasting love." Each word Ravneet shared was immersed in sheer admiration for the lady who touched the lives of everyone around with her boundless generosity, the pride of Punjab, Surinder Kaur.

All these amazing stories about this unwarped personality, the Nightingale of Punjab, are so golden and sacred that they need to be preserved forever. Shouldn't I be grateful that I have the universe in my hands in the form of the pen and He has chosen me to inscribe the story of *'The Complete Woman – Surinder Kaur'* whose life is inspired by the golden illumination of the sun that never dies.

8. SPRINKLING OF MOMENTS

Surinder Kaur desired and attempted to learn and speak English. She possessed the knack of picking up languages rapidly and that's the reason she could sing pretty effortlessly in Marathi, Bengali, Dogri, Pothohari, Pashtuni, Russian and Chinese too. Yet English was one vernacular that really troubled her. Years back, one fine evening Dolly asked her mother, "Mama, you have been to England, America, and Canada innumerable times. I wonder how you communicate with the people there." Surinder's soft lips stretched into a smile and she replied, "I have learnt a few words from your Daarji like *I see, really, certainly, responsibility, profession, etc. Meinu ehna di tune aaoundi hai*." On hearing the reply, Dolly found herself laughing so hard that tears clustered in the corners of her eyes, threatening to spill over.

Another desire that dwelled in Surinder's heart was to visit her birthplace. Her visit to Pakistan was preceded by a very interesting incident. Dolly was performing in Pittsburgh. During the concert, she received a piece of paper. She assumed it was a request for a song, but it turned out to be a request by someone called Z.A. Chaudhary who wanted to personally meet her after the concert. "After the performance, an elderly couple came to me, and the man handed me a small packet and asked me to unwrap it. It was a photo album with pictures of a house that I could not identify," Dolly recalls. Chaudhary then told her that it was her mother's parental house at Lahore which had been allotted to them after the Partition.

Three Generations

"From Pittsburgh, I went straight to New Jersey where Mama was staying with one of my sisters. I presented her the album. Mama opened it and wasn't she overjoyed!!! There was major excitement that night as Mama went over picture after picture recalling the old times. The stills had soaked her entire being and the mere sight of her home in Lahore was a salve to her wearied soul," added Dolly.

Once a newspaper reporter had asked Surinder if there was any unrealised wish of hers. And she told him that it was to go back to Lahore once and see the home she was born in. That desire of hers materialised when Surinder went with a cultural delegation to Pakistan. "I visited my house there. The street is still named after my father and called Bishan Street. Our house is still named after my mother; it bears the plaque 'Maya Bhawan.' It was strange, being there again after so long. Despite how long I'd been away, I still remembered everything about the place; the blue hydrangeas planted in the front yard, the soft tinkling of the wind chimes that reminded me of summer afternoons. The paint had faded since I had last seen it but I still recognized it. It looked like the colour of the sky before a bad storm. My friends/classmates were beyond excited to embrace me and chatter. They gave me so much love. And I sang my heart out to them as never before," Surinder had poured her heart out in one of her conversations with a media person.

What struck one as one visited her home was that Surinder lived with contentment of a life well sung. There was a library full of books of her husband. Her own awards lay scattered around. She literally had awards by the dozens including the Sangeet Natak Akademi award, Padmashri and the Punjab Sangeet Natak Akademi award. Most of the awards were kept dusted and polished by Paan Dev and his wife. "My greatest award has been the appreciation that I have got from my listeners," she always said. For summers she usually went to her daughters Nandini and Pramodini in New Jersey. Her home behind was taken care of by Paan Dev, his wife and their son whose education was backed by the lady herself. Paan Dev worshipped Surinder Kaur, "She has been my mother and she arranged and bore the expense for the marriages of my three daughters," he would often say to anyone and everyone who questioned him about Surinder Kaur.

It was Dolly's heartfelt desire to celebrate her mother's 75th birthday majestically, with grandeur and opulence. Artists from all around the globe came over to pay their regards to 'The Mother of Punjab'. The celebration began with a lullaby in Dolly's voice which her mother hummed years back when she put her firstborn to sleep. Upon listening that a lone tear traced down Surinder's cheek and in no time the floodgates opened. The beads of water started falling from her eyes one after another, without a sign of stopping. The tears made wet tracks down her face and dripped from her trembling, wobbly chin.

The best part of the evening was that it was a complete surprise for Surinder Kaur, although she could smell something dubious when her daughters Nandi and Baby came over especially for the day from the US. HMV Company honoured Surinder Kaur with lifetime achievement award and released an album, 'Solid Gold'. Her family gifted her a bouquet of 75 flowers. There was so much happening that day that most of the time her face seemed washed blank with confusion and amazement, as if her brain cogs couldn't turn fast enough to take in the information and pleasure from her wide eyes. Every muscle of her body just froze, before a grin crept on her face which soon stretched from one side to the other showing every single tooth of hers.

When Surinder Kaur moved to her new abode in Panchkula, her daughter – Dolly Guleria and her son-in-law, Sharanjit Singh Guleria made every possible effort to be by her side in the evening of her life. "It wasn't for mama…it was for my own self… because she was my harbour, an anchor I held onto for warmth, security and consistent love. I wanted to spend as much time as I could with her. I went over to her place every morning for a yoga session, returned home for a quick shower and then we both would sit together for our daily *riyaaz*. Many a times during *riyaaz,* her tears burst forth like water from a dam, spilling down her face and like a distressed child she would look at me and say, '*Doll, hun mere ton gaaya nai jaanda…mein thak jandi aa…galaa vi kuch sakht jeha ho gaya hai…bara zor lagauna painda hai…mein nai gaana…tu gaa…*' I would return to my home a hundred times in a day for sorting my household chores but my mind and heart would constantly be with Mama. I remember one evening when I went back to her, she lay on bed wholly immersed in watching a television serial that she hardly noticed me step into her room. And when she did, she got up all of a sudden and said, '*Tu kadon aayi doll.*' I wrapped my arm around her shoulders and pulled her close gently rubbing her arm. In that embrace, we both were cocooned and safe. Every time I hugged Mama, all my worries instantly disappeared like rain on summer earth. I said, '*Mama, TV dekhde raho... acha serial hai.*' I sat near her and started massaging her legs when I noticed her swollen feet. In no time she sat upright and in a reprimanding tone she said, '*Chadd mere pairaan nu.... Ethe mere kol palang te aa ke baith, ehna nu naa vekh...eh koi navii gal nai hai. Eh te rabb walo hi sujje hoye ne...ehna di bantar hi eho jahi hai...sair kerdi aa mein.. asal ch her samay safar ch pair latka ke hi baithe rehan naal pairaan di shape hi eho jahi ho gayi hai...*' Such was my maa... She had an explanation and answer for everything," reminisced Dolly Guleria. "I still remember when Maa would return home after performing, she would stroll leisurely in her strikingly manicured lawn reciting '*THE JAAP*'. At times she would recite it 108 times for my son Perry, at other times she would do so 108 times praying for the well-being of each member of her family. I can vividly recall *Paasho/Prakash Maasi's* daughters would call Mama and often request, '*Surinder Maasi, tusi saade lai vi ardaas kariyo.*' Each member of my immediate and extended family was of the opinion that Mama's prayers were unadulterated and unblemished, and that's the reason they reached God, surely and securely," Dolly continued.

Dolly's moist eyes (whenever she talks about her mother Surinder Kaur) are witness that she has been running endless emotional marathons on her bleeding knees. To me, Dolly Guleria looks like those leaves fluttering in the garden reflecting soft sun rays today. In the light of the day, one could never tell of the storm they had suffered a night before, of the winds that howled and tore their brethren from branches to ground, the subtle 'tells' of the 'Loss' they have faced. When I talked to her about her mother, in her eyes I could see and in her words I could feel the emotional debris of the grief hurricane that changed her life altogether, when she lost her anchor – her Mama…

9. TU VIDAA HOYON, MERE DIL TE UDAASI CHAA GAYI

Haaye ni meri amriye,
Hun kehre paase jaaiye,
Kehnu ro ro haal sunaaiye,
Ghup hanera koi raah naa disey,
Teinu kitho morr liaye......

(The above lines are from a song – a tribute to Surinder Kaur after her demise, penned by Jagmohan Sangha, composed and sung by Dolly Guleria at a show by PTC channel in front of a gathering of 15,000 people in Chandigarh)

22 November 2004

It was a bitterly cold morning. Surinder Kaur stepped out of the shower feeling cold and was handed over a glass of hot milk with a sip of brandy in it. Her facial expression changed while consuming it and within minutes she collapsed. Surinder's son-in-law, Sharanjit without wasting a moment, took her to the nearest doctor, who promptly said, "Take her to the hospital as soon as possible. It seems like a paralysis attack. At this stage, CT Scan is a must." Within minutes she was admitted at the Panchkula Hospital.

Surinder's physiotherapy sessions started as soon as she returned home. Many a times she became 'an exhausted unhappy' version of herself and would say, "*Meinu pata hai doll... mein hun es bimaari ton baad kadi America nai jaa sakdi*" and Dolly would hug her tight affectionately and optimistically say, "*Maa, tusi bahut jaldi theek ho jaana hai...pher aapan dovein America chalaangey... saareyaa nu mil ke aavangey...*" And it was destined to happen. After around six months, on 20 June 2005, both Dolly and her mother flew to the United States.

Life got back to normal when the mother-daughter duo returned to India. During the interview sessions then with the various media houses, Surinder often spoke loud and clear about her single regret and resentment. She said, "*Punjab Sarkaar ne meinu unj nai nawaazeyaa jivein mein apni zindagi Punjab te Punjabiyat te niyochaavar keeti hai...mein kadi neevein padarr de yaa ashleel geet nai gaaye... beshumaar ustaadan kolo achiyaa cheesan sikh ke peish keetiyaa per ehna kyo meri kadar nai paai.*"

The next year, 2006, began on an extremely positive note. Surinder Kaur personally went to Delhi to receive the coveted Padma Shri, the fourth highest civilian award. Even when she received the award, she was regretful that the nomination for the same had come from Haryana and not Punjab for which she worked tirelessly for more than five decades.

The year which had commenced with optimism and happiness, suddenly turned rough in April. Surinder's three upset daughters stood by her bedside trying to figure out the best for her in terms of her health. Nandi and Baby were adamant and insisted on taking her along to the United States for better medical treatment. Surinder Kaur herself seemed convinced and so on the 3rd of May, the three flew to New Jersey.

OHNE IK UDAARI AAISI MAARI,
OH MURR WATNI NAA AAYI...

After playing hide and seek for over a month, the legendary Surinder Kaur finally surrendered her defenses on 14 June 2006.

Dolly's entire world collapsed with the news of her mother's demise. She seemed encased in a cocoon, a bubble, alone and there was no way out. The wind died, the leaves ceased to rustle. Everything came to a standstill... She was surrounded by hundreds of people who came over to her place to mourn the death of her mother, yet she felt 'the loneliest'.

MAA TU MERI HOND HAIN...
MAA MEIN TERA PARCHAAVAAN......

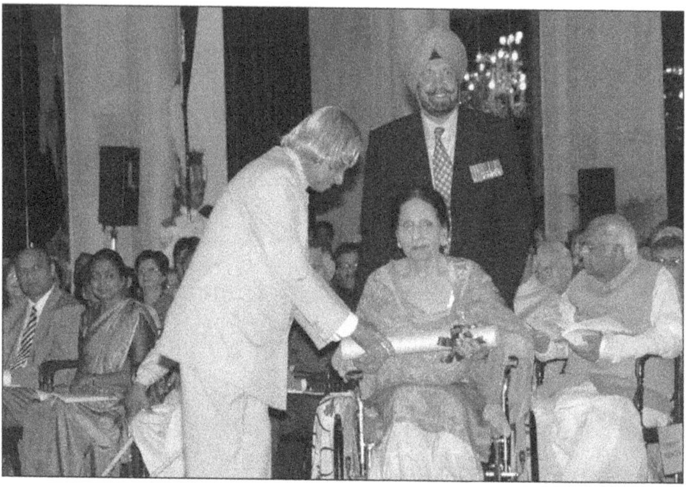

ABOUT THE NIGHTINGALE OF PUNJAB

1. Maa tujhe Salaam!

Mothers are extremely special souls. Much has been written about their character, their unmatched affection for their off-spring and so much more. My Maa, the simplest of the simple soul, who only knew the word 'Love' could sacrifice herself for the sake of those she loved. A lady with a heart of gold. No qualms of stardom hovered around her. An extremely down to earth artist who chose to mingle with her fans as any other normal being. Mama dressed like a true Punjaban with a style she designed for herself. She hated artificiality. She wore very few ornaments to enhance her beauty.

Mama had chiselled Aryan features which attributed to her charm. She learnt music from great maestros of her period and developed a style of her own. She sang every word of her song with understanding and gave her best self to it. She was an inspiration to millions of young talents through her mystical voice and rendition. Mama was elegance personified. She walked on the stage gracefully like a queen. She has left a void in the lives of all her fans but her music will live on till eternity. I am blessed to be the daughter of the legendary Smt. Surinder Kaur.

– **Dolly Guleria (Surinder Kaur's daughter)**

2. PUNJABI GEETAAN DI MAA

If Punjab had a face, it would be just like Surinder Kaur ji's. If Punjab had a voice, it would sound like Surinder Kaur ji. The most soulful, unblemished, pure voice that can touch the inner cords of each and every Punjabi, was, is and would forever be – Surinder Kaur ji's. *Asi khushnaseeb haan ke saade hissey aaisi fankaara aayi, jehna di paakeeza, bedaag, khuda daat aawaaz, sunan waleyaa de dil o dimaag nu dho gayi, paak ker gayi…ik aaisi aawaaz jo lukai de haan di hai…Ohna di khaali keeti jagah kadi poori nai ho sakdi. Haalan ki ohna di beti, Dolly Guleria, gaundi hai te dhee di awaaz cho maa di mehek aaoundi hai…Mein ik adney jahe fankaar di haisiyat naal jithe Surinder Kaur ji nu sajda kerda haan, othe naal naal dil ton shukar guzaar haan – Preet da, os di soch te os di kalam da, jo saada virsa akhraan ch quaid ker sambhaal rahi hai.*

– **Hans Raj Hans (renowned singer)**

3. THE KOYAL OF PUNJAB

'The Koyal of Punjab' was a complete package of immense knowledge, unpredictable creation and unmatched capability. In other words, Surinder Kaur ji was a university in herself. Her ability to translate the lyrics through her melodies has been unparalleled. From expressing her young exhilaration in '*Munda Lambarhan Da*' to telling the story filled with sorrow in '*Loki poojan rabb*', she has been exceptionally versatile and expressive of the entire range of emotions a human mind can fathom. In retrospect to her trilling and lightning-fast '*Murki*' and structural, laidback but touching vocals, it was her classical skills that she acquired through her learning experience under Ustad Abdul Rehman Sahab which she then gifted to the commercial Punjabi musicality. Ustad Panna Laal Kathak ji's compositions were just empty without her mesmeric voice. It felt that it was just her soul-stirring voice that was meant for Shiv Batalvi's words. I was given the privilege to call her 'Maa' by herself. I am very blessed that I have spent so much of my time with her and out of those beautiful moments, sharing an unforgettable one here.

It was her concert in my city Khanna, and I was invited as an honorary guest at that very event, with the badge of honour and everything! We all sat down, waiting for her and behold, Surinder Kaur ji came glistening on stage and started singing her heart out. Unfortunately though, the keyboard player was not at par with her abilities, no one can be. It was affecting her performance and I could not see that happening but I could not do anything either!

All of a sudden she stopped singing, looked at me and said, '*Sardool Beta, are you going to sit there as a guest of honour and just watch this happening or you're actually going to come up on stage and save me from this?'* A moment of silence because everyone was confused and shocked about what had just happened. *'Come and play the keyboard*!' She said and it was like I was just waiting for her permission. I ran up the stage, took the badge off and played throughout the concert.

I will never forget the day because out of every musical maestro sitting in the audience, she called me up and told me to play. She had the right over me and I feel fortunate about that.

Surinder Kaur ji treated me like her own son and I was blessed to have her; everyone was in this musical world. Artists like her are born after a thousand centuries and they end up being immortalized through the brilliance in their artistry. Maa still lives through her records, her memories and her art.

Bibi Surinder Kaur ji was, is, and forever will be the long-standing Queen of the Golden Era of Punjabi and Indian Music.

– **Sardool Sikander (eminent Punjabi singer)**

AMRITA PRITAM – THE WOMAN WHO DARED

AMRITA PRITAM

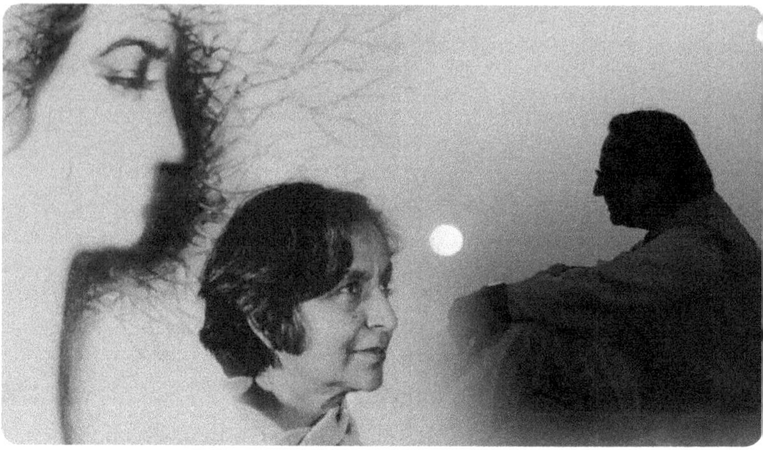
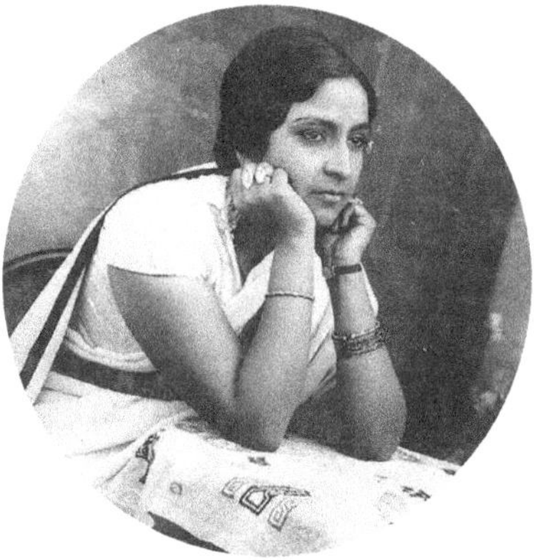
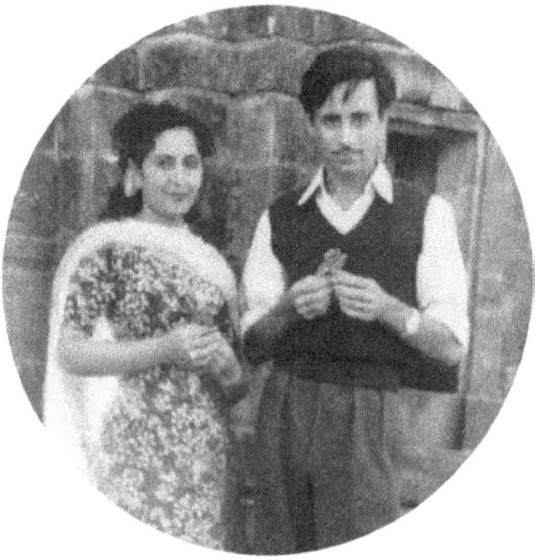
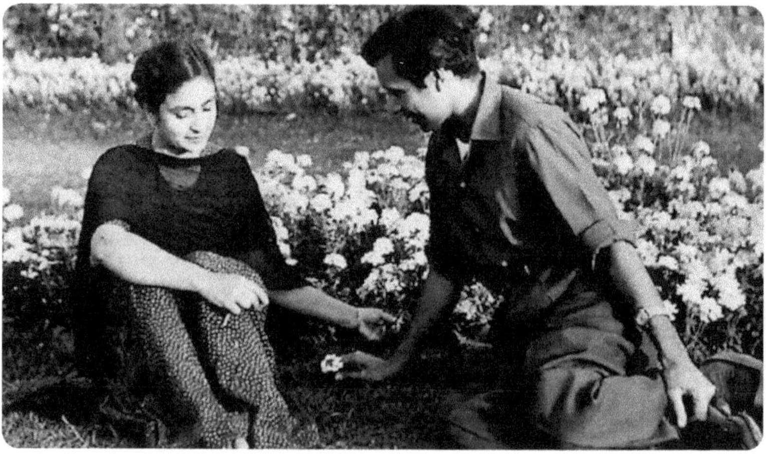

I emerged as a rebel who grew up absorbing pity of the society on my father for having five daughters. My schooling and the ambience I grew up in, fostered me with a resolute mind, and right from a tender age, the only person whom I looked up to and whose writings kept stamping over my heart since the day I first read her work, 'Kammi and Nanda', is Amrita Pritam. The Class VIII Hindi textbook published by NCERT (National Council of Educational Research and Training) in the eighties had a chapter which was from one of her works and had been translated from the original Punjabi into Hindi. That was my introduction to Amrita Pritam and her work. Manto and Khushwant Singh have also written about partition, but Amrita was a young woman in 1947, and the impact of seeing the violence which occurred then through the eyes of a woman is much, much more.

Amrita, for me, is revolution personified, a feminist before feminism, a firebrand poet and an agnostic. Love and defiance went hand in hand for this precocious poet. I have always found Amrita Pritam fascinating and immensely inspiring, and I have my reasons for that... One, because she was the first feminist writer Punjab ever had. Second, because she strove to give Punjabi women an identity and voice that went beyond conventional narratives. Third, because she held her views against narrow-minded, gender discrimination. Fourth, because she embodied the fullness of poetic expression, creativity and the intensity of a woman in the perpetual state of love. And last but not the least, because Amrita dared to live life – vividly and on her own terms.

Although I have grown up in her presence yet I am able to understand more of Amrita now. As of today, when my kids are off to universities, I get to spend more time with Amrita, Firaq and Faiz than I did in the yesteryears. The impact of her writings on me is such that today I have embraced the cloak of solitude. I perform my regular chores all day, be it at home or at professional front, and in the evenings I am abducted by the poems and writings of Amrita Pritam. Each evening I sit still in my home frontier, my leg crossed over my other ankle, with her writings in my hand. Each word penned by her is unique and this 'uniqueness' arises because of her foray into both lovely and harsh imaginative world which, apart from being confessional outpouring of a sensitive soul, is also a reflection on the patriarchal social constrains. And she speaks to me, so intimately as though she has waited for me forever. Today, through her writings she has become my friend and confidante. Her magic permeates the soft and deep hues of dreams, infatuation and longing. Every evening she walks into the recesses of my heart blowing away reticent cobwebs with her easy rustic Punjabi dialect. When I read her poems, I picture her talking to me in a warm tone. Her words do not leave me even when her book does. They are accessible and timeless for me. Amrita's verses have the redemptive grace of the Holy River as she flows ebulliently through my mind-locks and washes away all the scars of distress.

Yes! Amrita, my friend "*Mein teinu pher milaangi*/I shall meet you again" (surely next time in person) and perhaps, together we will wake up Waris Shah from his grave and implore him to write the devastating narrative that marred our land in 1947 during the partition. The effects of that fracture of partition are still reverberating in the mountains of Kashir...

Aj aakhaan Waris Shah noon
Kiton qabran wichon bol,
te ajj kitab-e-ishq da koi
Agla varka phol

2. ALL IN HER GENES

Once upon a time, 20-year-old Raj Bibi offered her homage at the habitation of sadhus of Gujranwala and there she saw Nand Sadhu. Nand Sadhu was the son of a wealthy money lender. When he was just six months old, his mother Lachmi died. Nand had four brothers and a sister. Two of his brothers had died. One – Gopal Singh – an inveterate drunkard, forsook his family for the love of the bottle. The other, Hakim Singh, took to the life of a sadhu. So Nand knew only his elder sister, Hakko, whom he loved dearly. Hakko wasn't happy with her marriage so she took the saffron robes and Nand followed her. Alas! His sister didn't live long and when she died Nand renounced the world.

Raj Bibi was from village Monga in Gujarat district and was married through the barter system but the man she was married to, got himself recruited as a soldier. Nobody ever heard of him again. She started teaching in a school at Gujranwala. One day it was raining heavily, Raj Bibi and her sister-in-law were forced to take shelter in an *ashram*. Nand Sadhu, with his eyes closed, was reciting some poems there. As soon as the recital got over and Nand opened his eyes, he saw Raj Bibi. He could not take his eyes off her. It was for her that he gave up his saffron robes and soon married her.

Raj Bibi and Nand Sadhu were destined to be parents of their only child, who was to become an important voice of Punjabi literature in the days to come. On his marriage, Nand changed his name to Kartar Singh. Since he wrote poetry, he had also taken on the pseudonym – *Peeyookh* – the Sanskrit word for nectar. Ten years later when their daughter was born, he named her 'Amrita', the Punjabi equivalent for *Peeyookh*, while he himself changed his *nom de plume* to Hitkari.

In her two autobiographical works *Kaala Gulab* and *Rasidi Tikat*, Amrita traced the development of her identity as a woman. Perhaps, that identity began with what she called 'one of nature's secrets' – a moment before her birth, when two little girl students of her father prayed publicly in the gurudwara: "Oh lord of the two worlds, may a little girl be born in the house of our masterji." Amrita's father was annoyed because he thought his wife must have known that the girls were going to pray in this manner. But later, the girls said that the prayer was their idea. If they had asked Raj Bibi, she might have wished for a son, but they wanted a baby girl – a girl like themselves. And so on 31 August 1919, Amrita was born in Gujranwala – a girl desired by two girls – later to give expression to the desires and feelings of many girls and women.

According to the archetypal theory, the self is made up of the elements inherited from the father and the mother. Having taught Amrita all he could about rhyme and rhythm, Kartar Singh's desire was that his daughter should find expression in poetry. So she began writing at a very early age. All she wanted at that time was to please her father. The love for literature and books came directly from her father. Should a page from a book be found on the floor, he would pick it up with solemn respect. Should by any chance Amrita's foot step on it, he would be extremely annoyed. Thus had been deeply engrained in Amrita's mind – respect for every written word – and with that for all those who wield the pen. The portrait of her father's Guru, Dayalji – the rare scholar of Sanskrit, hung at the head of her father's bed. Even to sit with feet stretched out in the direction of that portrait was forbidden. Amrita inherited both asceticism and worldliness from her father and had a streak of spirituality in her personality.

Self-respect is yet another quality that she inherited from her father. Her first book of poems appeared at the age of sixteen, and she received an award of a sari from the Maharani of Nabha and two hundred rupees from the Maharaja of Kapurthala by post. When the postman came the next time, she rushed to the door in anticipation of another award. Her father frowned upon seeing this and that frown of his accompanied her all her life. Never did she run after prizes or honours in her life – the love of her readers was the only thing that she always valued.

3. THE BIRTH OF A REBEL

Amrita was hardly eleven when her mother, Raj, suddenly fell ill. Barely a week later, with pale drawn faces, friends and relatives gathered at her bedside. "Where's my Binna?" she had enquired. By the time her friend Pritam Kaur got Amrita near her mother, she had lost consciousness. "Pray to God... Maybe the Almighty will show mercy... The child's prayers never go unheeded..." the good lady advised Amrita.

From her very young days, Amrita had learnt the art of disciplined meditation. Praying at that moment seemed a regular exercise. Little Amrita closed her eyes and folded her hands for a simple prayer, "Babaji, please don't let my maa die."

Although Raj Bibi bore her illness calmly, there was general bewilderment among those around. Baffled Amrita couldn't comprehend the entire scenario because she was extremely sure that God did listen to the prayers of the children. But death, like a shadow, lurked in the dark and crawled under the bed of her mother and gently took her away… far, too far to ever come back again. Everyone wept and wailed. Amrita took a final glance at her mother and burst out in red, hot wrath. "He, up there, doesn't exist… There is no God," she shrieked

From that day onwards, Amrita gave up all meditation and prayers she had been brought up with. Her father did not approve of all that and became sterner, but she was vehement in her resistance.

"There is no God…"

"Stop saying that Amrita."

"Why?"

"Because He has ways of showing his annoyance."

"Let Him… How can He when He isn't there?"

"And how can you be so sure?"

"Wouldn't He have heard me had He been anywhere?"

"What did you say?"

"I said, 'Please God, don't let my Maa die.'"

"But when did you see Him? He's invisible."

"That's fine… But can't He hear? Is He deaf?"

Amrita's father was immensely upset with her attitude. At times, he would take her by her shoulders and force her to sit down cross-legged to pray, with the command, "Shut your eyes and concentrate for ten minutes." But giving in to physical defeat only made her seethe with anger inside, "I have closed my eyes as you ordered Dad, but what can He do to me if I don't concentrate?"

"Yeh zindagi ek raat thi...hum toh jaagte rahe, kismat ko neend aa gayi..."

Amrita was born a rebel, a questioner of norms, and a devil's advocate of sorts. She asked difficult questions and challenged those things that everyone accepted as the norm. In her autobiography, she recalls that once as a young girl she noticed water being hawked at the railway platform as Hindu water and Muslim water. She questioned her mother – "*Is water also Hindu-Mussalman?*" Her mother's reply – "*It is this way here...*" – was not satisfactory for the young rebel. Later, a very young Amrita raised her voice against her conventional grandmother, who kept separate utensils for her Muslim visitors. It was "*...my first bagawat (rebellion) against religion,*" she wrote therein.

If Amrita silently rebelled against the father, she openly rebelled against the orthodox values of her grandmother. Amrita recalled an incident whenever her father's Muslim friends visited her house, they were offered tea in glass tumblers which were kept away from all other pots and pans on a shelf in the corner of the kitchen, in their 'ostracised niche'. The rebel in Amrita could not tolerate that and she revolted against this custom of her father and grandmother. Thereafter, not a single utensil was labelled 'Hindu' or 'Muslim' (The Revenue Stamp 5). She wrote, "Deep down in the layers of my mind, was the first impact of religion against which I had risen as a child when I had seen that glass tumbler touched by someone with a different faith became impure." (The Revenue Stamp 150).

Amrita shared her feelings about being a rebellious individual right from her birth in one of her interviews. She opined, "My mother never failed in the slightest degree, to honour and obey my father's male will. But it has always seemed to me that just as Parvati collected all the dust from her body and moulded from it the figure of her son Ganesh, so also my mother collected all the anger from her mind and poured it into my infant being, while she remained without a particle of anger..."

Amrita often said that her own rebellion against unjust restrictions as a 16-year-old girl later entered into her sympathy with all the oppressed people of the world, whether in Nazi Germany or occupied Czechoslovakia. Similarly, from her understanding of the primary inequality between male power and female powerlessness sprung her criticism of all kinds of tyranny, whether at the domestic or the national level: "Maleness is that spirit which always desires to put others in fear of itself... It is, in essence, the same whether demonstrated by a man who has only one woman under his control or by a ruler who can command thousands. After all, this is only a difference in degree, a difference in circumstances and ability." (*Aurat..123)*

4. SIXTEENTH YEAR

The sixteenth year is the most precious and glorious but extremely turbulent phase of a youth's life. When the first flush of youth knocks at the heart's door, turmoil begins within. Ironically, however, it creeps into the mind and the soul stealthily.

Amrita described the first touch of love in the sixteenth year of her age: "Came my sixteenth year – like a stranger. Inside me, there was an awareness I could not explain... Like a thief, came my sixteenth year, stealthily like a prowler in the night, stealing in through the open window at the head of my bed..." (The Revenue Stamp 11).

From an early age, Amrita could sense a shadow walking along her side. She named him R*ajan*... Her house was full of books – most of them were about religion, about *rishis* and their meditation and how *apsaras* like Menaka and Urvashi seduced the meditating rishis. It was reading them that her sixteenth year broke through the age of her innocence...

Amrita grew into a pretty girl with almond-shaped eyes, fine features and a fair complexion. She was also petite, barely five feet tall. And precocious. She began composing poetry in her teens and every poem she wrote, she carried the cross of forbidden desires. Her sixteenth year established no attachment with her. It was a surreptitious relationship. Like Amrita, her sixteenth year too was petrified of her father. Probably that's the reason that every poem she wrote she tore to bits and appeared before her father like a blameless, submissive daughter. Not that he objected to her writing poetry, but he desired her to pen religious verses, orthodox and conventional in style... Amrita's very important year came, and life took a different meaning. It was the beginning of the rutted road of life with all its hairpin bends, its ups, and downs... It was also the beginning of curiosity, and Amrita questioned everything – parental authority, whatever had been preached to her, and the entire stratified social scheme. She was thirsty for life. She desired living in contact with the stars she had been taught to worship from afar. And what she got in return for all these questions and inquisitiveness was advice and restrictions, which fuelled her rebellion. Undoubtedly, every girl goes through this kind of phase but it happened to Amrita with three times greater impact. First, there was the gloominess of middle class morality, then the dosage of 'don'ts' were thrust down her throat (the scenario would definitely have been different had her mother been alive) and finally, there was this domineering presence of her father, a man of religion, who wanted her to be an obedient daughter...and there was Amrita in her sixteenth year bearing her cross like a pang of unfulfilled love. She was sixteen and the memory of that year crept into every stage of her life.

It was in this very year that Amrita was given in marriage to the son of a prosperous trading family, the Kwatras, who owned a popular merchandise store in Lahore's Anarkali Bazar. Amrita precisely recalls the night of her wedding ceremony in her autobiography '*Raseedi Ticket*'. That evening, she went upstairs on the terrace and cried her heart out in pitch black dark. Her father knew about her state of mind and followed her. She kept telling him again and again that she didn't wish to get married. But alas! Things went the way they had been planned and as per her father's wish, she got married to Pritam Singh.

Later, as a mark of respect for her husband, Amrita replaced suffix Kaur by Pritam to become Amrita Pritam. Barely 16, it was too early to choose a life partner, especially when one was a woman as iconoclastic as Amrita. Although she did get married, it was a marriage of convenience; love wasn't something she associated with marriage. It was far from a happy marriage. There was no connection between the two. Amrita lived in a world of words, books, poetry, far removed from the world her husband inhabited.

The distance between the couple grew into an avalanche in 1960. They could not work out living together. And so in 1963, they fixed a date when they would begin to live separately – 8 January 1964 to be precise and they stuck to it. The husband-wife drifted apart: he to revive his business which had been ruined by the partition of Punjab, she to continue her career as a poet and a writer of fiction.

5. SILENCES THAT NEVER BROKE

Wohh afsaana jisey anjaam tak laana naa ho mumkin,
Usey ik khoobsoorat morr de ker chorna acha…

An era that is solely dedicated to technology leaves little or no scope for creativity to evolve through any means. The 'convenient' communication apps like Whatsapp and Facebook have gnawed at people's desire to use pen and paper to express. The dominance of convenience has deeply overshadowed the sublimity of words, of pen and paper, of poetry, of confidences, of life. But there has been a time about which a lot of us are clueless, where silence spoke a thousand words, paper expressed the deepest emotions and the smallest memoirs were the most prized possessions of every lover.

In the 1940s, Lahore was in ferment. College students took to the streets with dreams of a free India, while poets, singers, dramatists and other artists provided narrative to the rebellious spirits. It came as no surprise then that Amrita Pritam, who had made a name in the literary circles of Lahore, fell for the young, strapping poet Sahir Ludhianvi, whose first work Talkhian, set the city on fire. In her twenties then, the Punjabi poet anchored a radio show, and the lyricist edited Adab-e-Lateef, an Urdu magazine.

The attraction between the two was instant, explosive, particularly for Amrita. She was delicately beautiful, the words flowing from her like music, sensitive and eager to experience life to its fullest. Sahir was tall and brooding, with the abrasive idealism of a generation that wanted to set the wrongs of the world right with his words. Was it any wonder that they would recognize a kindred soul when they set eyes on each other.

They were attending a *mushaira* (poetry reading). Amrita was married to Pritam Singh at that point, but love often fails to see socially-constructed relationships. It just happens, like it happened to Sahir and Amrita. Eyes met in a dimly-lit room and what started conventionally turned into a love story that left us with poems that we all find solace in when we're heartbroken. She was immediately smitten by him. "I do not know whether it was the magic of his words or his silent gaze, but I was captivated by him," wrote Amrita of the moment. It was a captivation that would morph into an obsession, a tortured love that would not find fulfilment nor solace nor release.

The *mushaira* ended only after midnight following which the guests bid goodbye to each other. The next morning they were supposed to go to the neighbouring township of Lopoki, from where a bus had been organized to take them back to Lahore.

However, the following morning they discovered that it had rained the previous night and the road they had to take to reach Lopoki had been rendered slippery and hazardous. Apparently, the sky had turned cloudy during the *mushaira* itself and it had started drizzling by the time the *mushaira* had drawn to a close. Amrita saw the hand of fate in all of this as she recalled in one of her interviews, "Now when I look back on that night, I can say that destiny had sown the seed of love in my heart which the rain nurtured."

Desperate to go to Lopoki, the guests made their way ahead cautiously. It was in these circumstances that Amrita experienced her love blossoming for Sahir. She writes: Walking at some distance from Sahir, I noticed that where his shadow was falling on the ground, I was being engulfed by it entirely. At that time, I didn't know I would spend so many years of my life in his shadow or that at times I would get tired and seek solace in my own words. Many of my poems were written in Sahir's love, but I never revealed the inspiration behind them publicly."

Over the course of attending several such *mushairas*, the acquaintance between the two grew into a mutual affection. It was by all reckoning the most unusual relationship. The two hardly ever spoke to each other, preferring instead to let silence define their association. "There were two obstacles between us – one of silence, which remained forever. And the other was language. I wrote poetry in Punjabi, Sahir in Urdu."

The lovers continued their tryst, defying borders. They went beyond lust or possession, beyond cultural demands or class differences. Her relationship with Ludhianvi unfurled in the letters they wrote to each other. He was in Lahore, she was in Delhi; between them, they built a bridge of words, confidences, and endearments. Although they both were deeply affected by the Partition yet the letters did not stop. When souls become connected, it doesn't matter what political or personal turmoil goes on in the external world. There is a connection that traverses all other problems. In her letters, it's obvious that Amrita fell headlong in love with Ludhianvi. She called him '*Mera shayar*', '*Mera mehboob*', '*Mera khuda*' and '*Mera devta*'.

It is indeed a travesty that the relationship between Amrita and Sahir, two doyens of literature, couldn't mature into anything more substantial, something that mirrored their beautiful individual contributions to prose and poetry. Yet, it is probably with Amrita that Sahir came closest, at least in his mind, to a long-term relationship, as revealed in a telling conversation he had with his mother. Akshay Manwani, the author of *Sahir: A People's Poet*, believes Amrita was the only woman who could have convinced Ludhianvi to give up his single status. In fact, Ludhianvi had once remarked to his mother after seeing her, "*Woh Amrita Pritam thi. Woh aapki bahu ban sakti thi.*" ("That's Amrita Pritam. She could have been your daughter-in-law.").

Sounds all romantic and poetic, doesn't it? To date, people still wonder what stopped these two wordsmiths from coming together. Well, like all unfulfilled love stories, the answer to that question would be that it was them. Like all unfulfilled love, they came so close to it but had to say goodbye.

On the rare occasions when they did meet, they sat in silence. Amrita Pritam recounts these meetings in her autobiography *Rasidi Ticket*. It seemed like the silence was an extension of her, sitting next to her. Sahir would keep smoking until the ashtray was full of half-smoked cigarettes.

And once he had left, the half-smoked cigarettes were all that Amrita had left of him. She would keep the ashtray carefully in her cupboard. When the yearning got too much, she would smoke the leftover cigarettes, pressing her lips exactly where his had been. When you know that your love will remain unfulfilled, you hold on to whatever you can. Amrita wrote of the habit of smoking in her autobiography:

"When I would hold one of these cigarettes between my fingers, I would feel as if I was touching his hands. This is how I took to smoking. Smoking gave me the feeling that he was close to me. He appeared, each time, like a genie in the smoke emanating from the cigarette."

A similar incident that spoke highly of their pious and conventional style of loving was when a Punjabi composer, Jaidev, and Ludhianvi were working together on the lyrics of a song at Sahir's residence. Jaidev noticed a dirty and used cup lying on the coffee table. He immediately suggested that it needed to be cleaned. "Don't you dare touch it," Ludhianvi shot back. "Amrita drank tea out of it the last time she was here."

Sahir was a bundle of contradictions, a complex man with a thousand flaws but that's what drew people near him. Amrita was proud of her love for Sahir, she never failed to express it in her verses and whenever she got an opportunity to speak about it, she never shied away. In her autographical work, 'Raseedi Ticket' she wrote, "Posing for a picture of me at work, I was asked to sit and write on a paper with a pen in my hand. When I saw the paper later, I realised that absentmindedly I had written Sahir, Sahir, Sahir across the sheet."

Amrita writes in her poem 'Ek Mulaqat', that she dedicates to Sahir, of their love which could have existed only in these silences. In this meeting of lovers, where they quiver like a poem, and one half of which sits in one corner and the other half in another, does this meeting ever happen? Sahir and Amrita lived in different corners of the country and their love was like the torn pieces of the same poem, never together, never apart.

"Saamne puri raat thi, par aadhi nazm ek kone mein simati rahi, aur aadhi nazm ek kone mein baithi rahi."

6. THE IMMORTAL PARTITION POEM AND NOVELLA

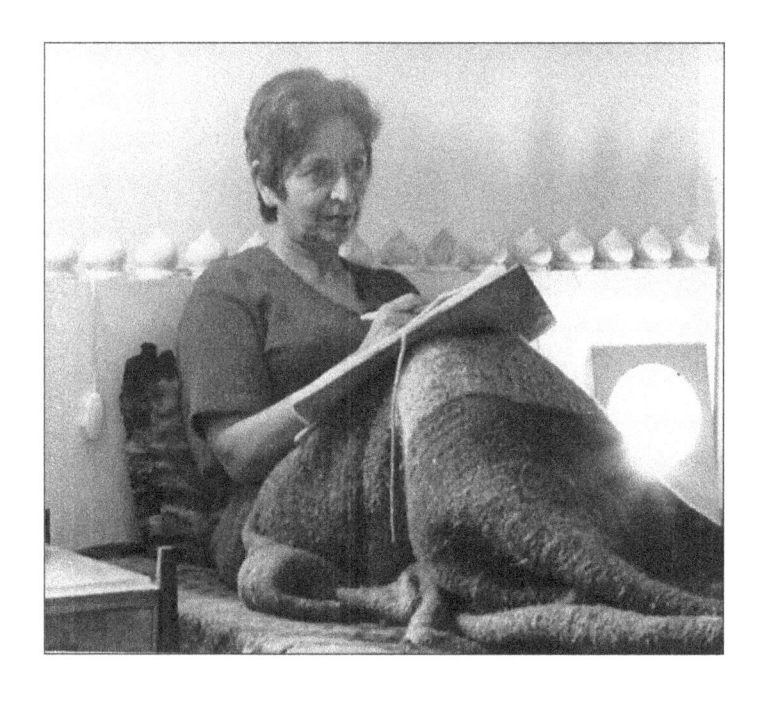

As a witness to Punjab's Partition, Amrita Pritam writes: "In 1947, Lahore was turned into a graveyard. It was the politics of hate that engulfed Lahore in flames; at night one would see houses being swept in flames, hear cries of pain, while the day would be spent witnessing long hours of curfew." Thus began her journey as a Punjabi refugee. She was 28 years old then. While travelling from Dehradun to Delhi, she wrote the *nazm* '*Aj Aakhaan Waris Shah nu*', on a scrap of paper. The poem turned out to be her signature tune. "But there were those who started abusing me in newspaper columns, castigating me on why I took up a Mussalman Waris Shah? The ones of Sikh faith asserted I should have written on Guru Nanak, while communists complained that I have ignored Lenin," she reminisces.

The train rolled through the dark night as though it was moving through a never-ending tunnel in the fall of 1947. A gloomy and gorgeous 'refugee' wondered if there would be light at the end of the tunnel, or whether she would keep travelling through the darkness, with her two little children by her side. Brave and daring always, the Punjabi Poetry diva was picking up shreds of life so that she could take root again. In her autobiography, *The Revenue Stamp,* she recalls the train journey thus:

"Uprooted from Lahore, I had rehabilitated myself at Dehradun for some time. I went to Delhi looking for work and a place to live. On my return journey in the train, I felt the wind was piercing the dark night and wailing at the sorrows the Partition had brought. I had come away from Lahore with just one red shawl and I had torn it into two to cover both my babies. Everything had been torn apart. The words of Waris Shah about how the dead and parted would meet, echoed in my mind. I thought a great poet like him alone could bewail the loss a *heer* once had to bear.

But who could lament the plight of millions of *heer* today? I could think of no greater than Waris Shah to chant my invocation to. In the moving train, my trembling fingers moved to describe the pangs I went through, and eventually my poem took birth."

ਅੱਜ ਆਖਾਂ ਵਾਰਸ ਸ਼ਾਹ ਨੂੰ ਕਿਤੋਂ ਕਬਰਾਂ ਵਿਚੋਂ ਬੋਲ।
ਤੇ ਅੱਜ ਕਿਤਾਬੇ ਇਸ਼ਕ ਦਾ ਕੋਈ ਅਗਲਾ ਵਰਕਾ ਫੋਲ।
ਇਕ ਰੋਈ ਸੀ ਧੀ ਪੰਜਾਬ ਦੀ ਤੂੰ ਲਿਖ ਲਿਖ ਮਾਰੇ ਵੈਣ।
ਅਜ ਲੱਖਾਂ ਧੀਆਂ ਰੋਂਦੀਆਂ ਤੈਨੂੰ ਵਾਰਸ ਸ਼ਾਹ ਨੂੰ ਕਹਿਣ।
ਵੇ ਦਰਦਮੰਦਾਂ ਦਿਆ ਦਰਦੀਆ ਉੱਠ ਤੱਕ ਆਪਣਾ ਪੰਜਾਬ।
ਅਜ ਬੇਲੇ ਲਾਸ਼ਾਂ ਵਿਛੀਆਂ ਤੇ ਲਹੂ ਦੀ ਭਰੀ ਚਨਾਬ।

Today, I call Waris Shah, "Speak from your grave"
And turn to the next page in your book of love,
Once, a daughter of Punjab cried and you wrote an entire saga,
Today, a million daughters cry out to you, Waris Shah,
Rise! O' narrator of the grieving! Look at your Punjab.
Today, fields are lined with corpses, and blood fills the Chenab...

What made her first poem after Partition most poignant was the fact that Amrita was an eyewitness to the horrors of Partition and also a victim. She was among the thousands who migrated from West Punjab to make their home across the fence. Her two most outstanding literary works are the Waris Shah poem, penned in winter after the bloody month of

August in 1947, and her novel Pinjar, which appeared in the early fifties.

The novel was too radical for its times because the wounds had not yet healed, and the communal hatred was still at its peak. Even in those difficult times, Amrita was able to write a novel that saw the situation from the point of view of the other. This emotional and heart-breaking novella fetched Amrita 'the La Route des Indes Literary Prize' from France for its French translation by Dennis Metrineje, in 2005. Earlier, the novel had been translated into English by Khushwant Singh and published with the title 'The Skeleton'.

Amrita's story of Partition, its horror and tragedy has man as the tormentor and woman as the sufferer. It focuses more on the trauma of women abducted, raped, murdered, stripped, paraded naked in the streets, forcefully married or made slaves by the opponent community. The most positive thing about the novel, unlike other Partition novels, is that 'Pinjar' ends with recognition, recovery and rehabilitation of the abducted women. As Bharti Ray quotes, Nehru too had made a strong public appeal: "I am told that there is unwillingness on the part of the relatives to accept those girls and women... This is most objectionable and wrong attitude to take and any social custom that supports this attitude must be condemned. These girls and women require our tender and loving care."

7. KAAGAZ TE CANVAS

Baap Veer Dost te khavind
Kise lafz da koi nahin rishta
Uj jadon mein tainu takkiyan
Saare akkhar gurhe ho gaye...

Born in the year 1926 in *Chak Number 36*, a village 100 kilometres from Lahore, Imroz met Amrita through an artist when she was looking for someone to design the cover of her book. "I had not seen her but read the book 'Doctor Dev' in which she had described what her man should be like. I was astonished to see the protagonist as my own reflection. I felt Amrita was introducing me to myself and my kin whom I had never met before. I was in love with her anyway, so I called her up (in 1957) and said, 'I am your Doctor Dev speaking' and put the phone down'." Imroz met Amrita in person five years later. It was only 12 years later that when she was complaining of crank calls, including the one Imroz had made, that he told her he had made it.

Amrita had a strong public persona – because she was a successful writer and because she chose to live life on her own terms. Imroz, however, perhaps temperamentally shy and reclusive, chose not to 'exhibit' (he dislikes the very word) his works in the professional art gallery domain. He, thus, remained somewhat of a shadowy figure looming on the fringes of Amrita's popular presence. After meeting her, he had so completely merged his identity with hers that he was always present but hardly ever noticed.

Walking down the memory lane, Imroz recounts how he met Amrita for the first time through a common friend. He lived at Patel Nagar (East) and Amrita at Patel Nagar (West). He was then working with an Urdu magazine, *Shama*. Amrita wanted him to make illustrations for her books. Cupid struck during their first rendezvous. *SHAMA* was a very popular magazine with a circulation of over a hundred thousand copies. Imroz's sketches brought to this monthly a fresh breeze of creativity. This magazine also opened new avenues for Imroz. He fondly recalls, "Guru Dutt noticed my work and asked me to do designs for his film *Pyaasa*. He liked my work for *Pyaasa* and later asked me to move to Bombay and work for him. I too wanted to move to Bombay. I went to meet Amrita, who herself was going through a rough phase in her personal life. Her marriage was withering away like a lifeless tree and her heart pined for Sahir Ludhianvi. Amrita's drifting hardship was desperately seeking an anchor. She just demanded three days from me. Three days of togetherness… It was the May of 1958 and we spent those three days walking and sitting in silence underneath the flaming laburnum trees with their flowers in full bloom and somewhere within the silent space of knowing the decision of spending our lives together was taken between both of us." Imroz embraced Amrita's two children – Navraj and Kundala and thus began a 40-year-old journey of supreme sacrifice and unconditional love. With the passage of time, their love flourished, though they never spoke of the 'love' they experienced for each other when they met. An unspoken emotion nurtured their relationship. "She never used to cook, but when she saw me first, she started cooking," reminisces Imroz, who used to write prose, but started writing poetry, post meeting his love.

"We never said 'I love you' to each other. It wasn't needed. What is love? Love is taking care of tiny things for each other. When we decided to live with each other, we didn't let anyone interfere with our decision. I told her, 'You are my society. I am your society.' And why do you call it live-in? Aren't others live-in relations?" Imroz shares...

While Amrita wrote her novels, wove her stories and was winning all the attention and awards, Imroz was the pillar of strength, the very ink that flowed through her pen, the muse that inspired many characters and the invisible rhythm to which her heart was always beating. Imroz shared Amrita's laughter, sorrows, deepest fears and he designed the jackets of her books and he also became the jacket that protected Amrita's soul. She confessed to her diary, "Imroz is my insulation from the outside world. He protected me from it all – the unwanted interruptions of the doorbell, the phone rings and visitors." Imroz was a shadow, a confidante, a dedicated friend, a lover and a fakir in most ways.

Egoless, self-assuming, a heart full of *ibadat* – a love that is any woman's dream.

To be honest, the first thought that came to my mind when I started reading, writing and exploring Amrita – the woman was 'a regret'. A regret of not having met her in person, but my loss of not being able to have a talk with Amrita was amply compensated for by the opportunity I got to speak to Amrita's constant companion, nay her alter ego, Imroz. Imroz, the artist, is the epitome of a real man. He is simple and humble yet suave and sensible. Amrita is fortunate to have enjoyed the companionship of a person like him, calm, placid and unperturbed.

"What did you like most of Amrita?" I questioned Imroz. "Her presence," he replied. I further asked Imroz, "How far is *The Revenue Stamp* a true picture of Amrita's life?" Imroz describes *The Revenue Stamp* as a stupendous achievement. "No other writer could be so bold in presenting himself or herself. It is a true image of her life." He said, "One needed vision to perceive her autobiography in right perspective."

Amrita celebrates her relationship with Imroz in *The Revenue Stamp*. He is 'The 15th August' for her. Her bereaved soul received the balm of love from Imroz. Her life-long quest for love ended in Imroz who fused meaning into her life.

Amrita and Imroz created collaboration on the other hand, gave birth to a beautiful child that was conceived in the womb of artistic expression – *NAAGMANI*...a magazine for the readers of fine Punjabi literature was born in 1966. "When the idea of *Naagmani* was conceived, prior to the readers, obstacles welcomed us. The top three publishers from Delhi refused to print it. But we didn't lose hope and embraced those difficulties too. Far away from our residence in Hauz Khas, towards the Sabzi mandi, was this very small press which printed odd and unimportant stuff. *Naagmani* was destined to be printed and hence the journey began from that tiny press," recalls Imroz, as if it was just yesterday that the journey of Naagmani began. This magazine became the full moon of the monthly literary calendar with readers desperately awaiting the next issue.

Furthermore in the 'Am-Roz/Amrita and Imroz' life, Imroz offered his share in each household chore. If Amrita scrubbed the dishes, Imroz helped her by heating and pouring the water for the washing and so on. When Imroz ran out of funds, Amrita bought all his pictures and offered him money to purchase new canvas. When the sales of Amrita's books were delayed and she was distressed, Imroz helped her and kept her morale strengthened. Amrita always prayed to get a partner like Imroz in her next birth also. Amrita and Imroz were two different selves with one soul...truly made for one another. They loved, respected, understood and took care of each other's freedom in a unique way without any social or religious bondage. Hey Amrita, as

I am penning the 'AM-ROZ' story, if I had to be hypocritical I would say, "Ah! What a love story... But to be honest, all I wish to say is 'Amrita, I envy you Lady.'"

Amrita's accident and her prolonged illness was the next chapter in their story. Imroz's love for Amrita remained as constant as the sun that entered their house in Delhi every day. He lit lamps of great hope and sat beside her while she laboured through the pain. Amrita's health took a downslide after she broke her pelvic bone after slipping in the bathroom in the winter of 2002. It was around that time that she decided to wind up Naagmani that baptised hundreds of people into the world of literature. In the subsequent years, her pain subsided but she could not walk again. She swung like a pendulum between hope and despair. As death stared at her, she wrote her touching swan song, '*Main tenu pher milaangi* (I will meet you again)', addressed to Imroz, taking their love onto a cosmic plane for an eternal reunion. At the fag-end of her life, she went into a long silence as if she intentionally withdrew her consciousness from this material world, well before she left this world on 31 October 2005.

The day Amrita's body was being consumed by fire, one is introduced to a stoic Imroz deeply in love still but detached. At the end of the deserted cremation ground, people were standing, silently staring at the burning pyre. Away from everybody, alone, standing in a corner, one could spot Imroz.

Ironically, poetry started flowing through Imroz only after her death. He wrote beautiful poems about her, which he could no longer read out to her. When asked, "Doesn't it hurt you? Don't you feel she should have been around to appreciate your poetry?"

He said, "I think it reaches her wherever she is now." Perhaps, they are meeting at the same cosmic plane she referred to in her last poem.

"Main jab khamosh hota hoon
Aur jab khayal bhi khamosh hote hain,
To ek halki halki sargoshi hoti hai
Uske ihsaas ki
Uske sheron ki." – by Imroz for his Amrita

Amrita might not be around, but she lingers on in Imroz's thoughts and reflections (besides that of her readers), each day, every moment. I thought of Victor Hugo: "Love is a portion of the soul itself, and it is of the same nature as the celestial breathing of the atmosphere of paradise." And for Amrita and Imroz Sahab, love did bestow an atmosphere of paradise, in which two souls strum together a ceaseless symphony of 'celestial breathing'. And its rhythm continues to nourish and nurture their relationship, offering an ode to the very idea of love.

"Let the joys and sorrows of life...yours and mine... mingle like waters from two rivers... And then, it would be difficult to separate your existence from mine just as no one can draw a line on water."

8. YEH TERA GHAR, YEH MERA GHAR

The country I presently live in – England, showcases the home of Shakespeare at Stratford-upon-Avon as one of the greatest national assets, whereas the country I was born in – India, allowed great Urdu poet Mirza Ghalib's home in Old Delhi to turn into a coal depot over the years. While Virginia Woolf's country retreat, where she wrote her best works is preserved by the National Trust, K-25, Hauz Khas, Amrita and Imroz's abode, from where came over

100 books by the author is nothing more than debris. It was a home that Amrita and her partner Imroz had built together literally brick by brick from their earnings. They shared it for nearly half a century and while she willed the house to her son Navraj, Amrita had spelt out that the first-floor be preserved as it is and Imroz be allowed to live there till the last breath. Imroz, who later made an effort to arrange her paintings, books, awards and other objects just as they were in the old home, says: "I did not let them demolish the nameplate. I brought it and now will frame it." When asked about the lost home he replied, "Everyone is shocked but the new generation will do new things. I had built this home with Amrita brick by brick and the relationship breath by breath. What has been demolished is a house; the home was our relationship."

What made K-25, Hauz Khas so special was that its doors were always open to all writers, and littérateurs visiting from Punjab would be given a place to stay in her library-cum-guest room and food cooked by her as long as she was healthy. One recalls a *mushaira* held on the terrace when Faiz Ahmed Faiz visited Delhi. Frequent visitors were Gulzar, Deepti Naval, Shabana Azmi, Sahir Ludhianvi, and other international who's who. Though readers do feel sad but not dejected because the grand dame of letters who is best remembered for her Partition poem 'Waris Shah I call out to you today...' had also written, rather prophetically:

Aaj main apne ghar da number mittaiya hai
Te gali de matthe de lagaa gali da naam hataaiya hai
Te har sadak di disha da naam poonj ditta hai
Par je tussa mainu zaroor labhna hai
Ta har des de, har sheher di, har gali da booha thakoro
Ih ik sraap hai, ik var hai,
Te jitthe vi sutantar rooh di jhalak paavey
.........samajhna uh mera ghar hai.

9. EMOTIONS CHAINED IN WORDS

The fact of a woman taking pen in hand was enough to raise eyebrows but when Amrita began to critically analyse marriage, the family and the unequal man-woman relationship, at a time when the dominant trend in Punjabi literature was to glorify woman as wife and mother, the Punjabi literary world stood up as one man to cry sham on her. In Amrita's words: "Society attacks anyone who dares to say that its coins are counterfeit. But when it is a woman who dares to say this, society begins to foam at the mouth. It puts aside all its theories and arguments, and picks up the weapon of filth to fling at her. A woman who has suffered an attack can understand it, this attack is not against a particular woman, it is an attack on the entire womankind... So my story is the story of women in every country and many more in number are those stories which are not on paper, but are written in the bodies and minds of women..." (Kaala Gulab, 71) All her life, Amrita had to contend with various forms of attacks. When her early poems were published and reviewed, her photograph appeared in some newspapers. There was an immediate uproar.

People said: "The pictures of respectable men's daughters have started being put up in paanwalas' shops and men's hostels." The fact of her being a woman was the prime weapon used against her. "My youth, my appearance, my womanhood were always put into the balances and weighed against every poem of mine." (Kaala Gulab, 71) She was accused of trying to get fame on the basis of her looks.

Amrita's own struggles as a woman are the life and breathe of many of her works. "When I could not call Amrita Amrita, I called her Nirmala or Achla, Malika or Karmawali, Ratni, Canny, Meenu or some other name..." (Preface to Aksharon Ki Chhaya Mein). With her seasoned craft of weaving a plot and creating motivated characters, her acceptance as a novelist was all-pervasive among the women. The lustre of her poetic expression in prose was a boost to her receptivity amongst readers of all ages, irrespective of the caste and creed they belonged to. Throughout her life, Amrita had been a symbol of liberation for contemporary women writers. Amrita has ardently highlighted man's disaffection with woman. A poem titled *Kunvaari* (Virgin) in her Jnanpith Award-winning *Kaghaz Te Canvas* depicts the modern girl as follows:

When I moved into your bed
I was not alone – there were two of us
A married woman and a virgin
To sleep with you.
I had to for the virgin in me
I did so

This slaughter is permissible in law
Not the indignity of it
And I bore the onslaught of insult.

Amrita has succeeded in presenting such themes with all the sophistication of a protagonist seeking to change social values. She has been in the forefront when it came to defying all that was outworn and obsolete in society. One may not agree with her solutions but one has to accept that her writings did set the ball rolling in so far as challenging wrongs in society was concerned.

Once, the great critic Revti Saran Sharma asked Amrita a notable question: "Amrita! If the heroines of your novels in search of truth leave their homes, don't you think the effect of it can be shattering in the social context, I mean?" Amrita replied, "If false social values have until now accounted for broken homes, let a few more be broken but, mark you from now on, at the altar of truth!" In a way Amrita's life itself is a long and painful search for truth. The same is true in the case of her heroines. There was no space for hypocrisy and snobbery in her life and in the lives of her characters.

In a literary career spanning seven decades, Amrita wrote 24 novels, 15 short-story anthologies and some 23 volumes of poetry, greatly enriching the Punjabi language. Amrita Pritam's works have been translated in English, Albanian, Bulgarian, French, Polish, Russian, Spanish and all the 21 Indian languages. She was the first woman to be conferred with the prestigious Sahitya Akademi award, for *Sunehray* ('Golden'), her anthology of Punjabi verse, in 1955.

She was also the first Punjabi woman to be awarded the Padma Shri, one of India's highest civilian awards in 1969 and won the Bhartaiya Jnanpith Award, India's highest literary award, for her anthology *Kagaz Te Canvas* (The Paper and the Canvas) in 1982. In addition to this, she received three D Lit degrees from Delhi, Jabalpur and Vishva Bharti Universities in 1973 and 1983 respectively. Amrita received International Vaptsarove Award by the Republic of Bulgaria in the year 1979 and the Shatabdi Samman – Millennium poet in the year 2000.

Amrita went on to become a Rajya Sabha member in 1986. All throughout, she continued writing of love and life with an insistence, as though she couldn't survive otherwise.

"I have just returned what I absorbed from reading the great poetry of the great Sufi and Bhakti poets of my land," Amrita has modestly said in one of her interviews.

10. AMRITA – THE PERSON

As I scanned Amrita's literary autobiography, I felt there are gaps and silences which need to be read into.

Amrita was a person of many parts. She was an extremely good conversationalist and could hold audiences of all shades. Whether she acquired this art from the stint she had with the All India Radio or she was picked up by them because of this talent in her is a matter of debate.

Amrita felt more at home with the *mazaars* of Mian Meer Waris Shah and Bulleh Shah which were as dear to her as the Taj and Roza of Ajmer Sharif. This did not apply to the places of worship of other religions in her case.

With all her honours and acclaim, the heights she reached in her lifetime, including the membership of the Rajya Sabha, bestowed on her by late Prime Minister Indira Gandhi, she carved out a niche for herself amongst the immortals of Punjabi literature. Born in the same year as Indira Gandhi, and perhaps under the same stars, consciously or accidentally, she waited for the same date to take leave of the world.

Shy of meeting people and visiting different places, Amrita was fond of cooking at home. Hundreds of visitors from other parts of the country and abroad would remember the lime tea served by her. Those interested in artistic calligraphy still continue to visit Imroz's and Amrita's home which is full of her writings inscripted by Imroz on all possible corners.

Four decades of her companionship with Imroz has enabled him to master the art of tea-making and one can be sure of Amrita's legacy being carried on by him.

Amrita Pritam did not confine herself to the limits and boundaries of this Punjab. She did not belong to either side of the Wagah border or even both sides put together. She was the voice of Punjabis all over the world and hence the voice of humanity.

Another aspect of Amrita was that as an iconoclast, she admired and supported the revolutionary thinking of Osho. She wrote the introduction for several books of Osho, including Osho's discourses on the *Japji Sahib* entitled – *Ek Omkar Satnam* and his most-talked about book, *From Sex to Superconsciousness*. Her statements about Osho showed her deep dimension of spirituality, for example, "Where the dance of Meera and the silence of Buddha meet, blossoms the true philosophy of Osho."

Being Amrita, wasn't an easy job... Amrita shared in one of her interviews that she had to go through many struggles and difficulties in life. After partition, she got a job with All India Radio. She had to stick to it for a full twelve years... For the first few years she had a daily contract of Rs. 5! Even if she had a cold or fever she could not miss a day. One of her colleagues, Mr. Kumar helped her a lot and gave her the shorter announcements by taking the longer ones himself. Amrita commented that, whatsoever life offered her, the one thing that did not let her down during the most depressing times was her 'Pen'. "There have been so many days when I have held my pen close to my chest and continuously wept..."

In spite of her individual and independent thinking, Amrita was never bereft of tender motherly feelings. She believed in the principle of sharing and not dominance. She always enjoyed her femininity and its various role patterns like daughter, mother and wife. She shared in her biography about her maternal feeling – the year 1969. She penned that a sudden trunk call of her son from Baroda University sent shivers down her spine. In reply to all the letters she had written, after a long time-span her son said on the phone, "I'm fine Mamma – in perfect health." Amrita very lucidly depicted her deeper feelings at this juncture. Listening to the ring, Amrita felt on cloud nine. She remarked, "My flesh melted into my very spirit and fed the pure naked soul to a flame... As lightning in the dark, a thought flashed across my mind if I, an ordinary woman, could get a mighty

ਤਾਇਆ ਜੀ ਦਾ ਪਿਗਲਾ ਘਿਸ਼ਨ ਚੇਹਰਤਾ ਰਿਗਤਰਾਰ

BHAGAT PURAN SINGH JI
1904 - 1992
Founder Pingalwara, Amritsar

EH JANAM TUMHARE LEKHE

DR. INDERJIT KAUR

Je Tu Pooran Bhagat Kahaavna, Pehlan Main Da Ghar Lai Dhaa,
Sab Bharam Bhulla De Ve Man'nah Te Fakar Joon Handah,
Mann'ah Sun Ve Pindeh Apne Kise Tanh Di Peedh Handah,
Chal Rooh V Dhoyie Apni, Kise Pindeh Pani Paa…
Sunn Ve Poorna, Rabb Kitte Door Na
Dukhaan Vich Jhoor Na, Te Kojhiya Nu Ghoor Na

Credit: Movie - Eh Janam Tumhare Lekhe,
Lyricist - *Raj Ranjodh*, Singer - *Diljit Dosanjh*.

ABOUT AMRITA

The contribution of Amrita Pritam to Punjabi letters is unparalleled. She touched so many genres of literature but it was as a poet she surpassed all. None of her contemporaries could write a poem like *Ajj aakhan Waaris Shah nu*. She translated world literature for the benefit of Punjabi readers and she encouraged young writers. If a poem or a story was good, she published it without caring if it was coming from a novice or a known writer. She was also a non-conformist. Even the most bitter of her critics have not been able to fault her for her gift to language and literature. They found other things to pull her down like her short hair, her cigarette, her romances and I would tell them that these would perish with her body but her spirit will live in her work. And so she lives on…entering the 101st year and will continue to do so…

– Dalip Kaur Tiwana
(Distinguished Punjabi writer)

thrill from the sound of my son's voice, what must Mata Tripta have felt during the time she was carrying Nanak?"

From the author of the Millennium Award to every title India could felicitate her with, she had trophies by the dozen but you would never see any of them on display at her home. What Amrita did keep close to her were paintings by the other great love in her life, Imroz, her partner, as humble as Amrita herself. Amrita Pritam was humility personified.

I come from a Sikh family but somehow I respect each religion yet no religion because for me, love and compassion have been my canon and precept. Probably that's the reason that Pingalwara, Amritsar and Unique Home, Jalandhar have been my places of worship.

Ironically, when I look around I see a world that has been so artistically composed whether purposely created by a higher form of being or by a scientifically interpreted big bang. But where is the beauty in living in a world composed, governed and preserved by humans who lack a sense of humanity? And, it saddens me…it saddens me that there are those who are just as human as you and me in their physical being but are not as human in terms of characteristics in which the term itself reflects. It saddens me to watch all that is living be abused by others that are equally human but unequally humane. It saddens me that our pure souls have been poisoned by greed that has become limitless in its ability to seek destruction. We have become masters of diffusion of responsibility, claiming to be humane and linguistically convincing ourselves and those dear to us that we seek change, the existence of a better world and the well-being of others whilst our souls and our *Karma* fail to reflect such pure intentions. It saddens me that we choose to sympathise only through a glass shield. Why? Because we have become masters of words and failures of actions.

WAIT…why do I sound so disconsolate? Why am I focussing on the 99 inhumane rather than highlighting the one empathetic, who despite being homeless himself became a home for thousands others… *Nithaanvyaan de Thaanv*… Bhagat Puran Singh ji, founder of Pingalwara, Amritsar…

As a child, once in a while when I accompanied my parents to the Golden Temple, Amritsar, I recollect Bhagat ji sitting at a shady spot on the *parikarma*, with dozens of books around him and loose sheets of paper scattered on the marble floor. Most of the time he would sit there silently, handing pamphlets to pilgrims who crossed him and then went back to his writing. During one such visit, I can hazily recall Bhagat ji getting upset with the *sewadaars* of the Golden temple who came near him with bucket full of water to wash the marble floor. He got dismayed seeing the criminal waste of one of our most precious resources.

In July 1992, Bhagat ji suffered a stroke and was shifted to the PGI at Chandigarh and on 5th of August, at 2:30 pm, the bearded Mother Teresa of Punjab passed away. In his last days, Bhagat ji was overly anxious about the future of Pingalwara. Before leaving, he made sure he handed over the reins of 'His temple of humanity' in the right hands. He was confident that his *moonh boli dhee,* Dr. Inderjit Kaur, who was compassion and empathy personified, would nurture the flame lit by him. And she has not let him down. Dr. Inderjit Kaur has been an epitome of self-sacrifice and self-abnegation. For her, the service of mankind has been a constant flow of spirituality. Bibiji is a shining example for the world to emulate.

When the concept of this book was conceived, the first name that hit my mind was – Dr. Inderjit Kaur's, a virtuous soul, who has been a role model for me like millions others. Pingalwara is a metaphor of help in a world full of misery. This institution has grown and become the centre of the service movement under the able guidance of Dr. Inderjit Kaur and through her selfless service 'The Sage of Pingalwara' continues to live…

2. THE STORY BEGINS

This is the story of a shade tree, whose spreading canopy and crown is providing shelter to innumerable penurious and impoverished wanderers from sunlight in the heat of the summer. This is the tale of 'The Humanitarian' who emerged as an epitome of empathy and compassion. This is also the story of the girl who took three major courageous decisions in her lifetime which changed her life and the lives of thousands of castaways of society: the sick, disabled and abandoned forlorn people. This is the story of the lady who is carrying the torch of selfless service lit by the saintly hero – Bhagat Puran Singh ji and serving as the *Mukh Sewadaar* of the Pingalwara Charitable Trust. This is the story of Dr. Inderjit Kaur…

Inderjit Kaur, who has never visited Gujranwala area of Pakistan, yet her eagerness touches its zenith whenever somebody mentions about that place because that's where her ancestors belonged to. Her grandfather – S. Shivdayal Singh, a tender-hearted business man died very young because of the epidemic of plague. His widow Kesar Devi, had just one burning desire – to impart the best possible education to her children. Her eldest daughter, Kartar Kaur, was unable to receive proper formal education, which remained Kesar Devi's only regret for her entire life. She sent her son, Harbans Singh to study in Lahore whereas her youngest daughter, Shanta, was admitted in the nearest school which was around four miles from their village. A *'kachcha'* road led to that school with no transport facility of any sort available. All these hurdles could not dampen Kesar Devi's spirit because her resolution seemed staunch. She would accompany her daughter to school in the morning and then return to her village after dropping her off and would cover the same distance again to fetch her daughter back from school. In totality she walked 16 miles a day chasing her dream of seeing her children well versed and educated.

After completing his school education, Harbans Singh joined Ayurvedic College. Where on one hand the entire village was pleased with S. Shivdayal's son's accomplishment, on the other hand they couldn't digest the fact that the daughter of Shivdayal Singh also had joined the Medical College, Amritsar.

Harbans Singh was in awe of his mother. Her ability to cling together (as a family and as a part of the community) when trials were heavy and endeavour by her kind precepts and counsels to dissipate the clouds of darkness and cause peace to return to the hearts of one and all, was something which gave him strength and a goal too. This was the foremost reason that he opted to open his Ayurvedic practice in Sangrur in the year 1930. His sister, Shanta, too had completed her L.S.M.F by that time and got a govt. job. She was posted at Dalhousie in Gurdaspur district. Later on, she was transferred to Majitha in 1947 and had just settled there when she was transferred to Shakargarh in Sialkot district that became a part of Pakistan. As the madness of partition and riots spread all over, it wasn't safe for her to serve at that place. Hence she resigned. On the other hand, there was considerable shortage of doctors in Rajasthan. The Maharaja of the princely state of Rajasthan personally came over to see and convince Shanta to join his state to which she agreed and was posted at a place known as Kotputli in Tikana state. The amount of affection and admiration the people of this state showered upon her in lieu of her dedication and commitment of her work propelled her to settle down at this place for good. Shanta's mother was worried about her daughter's future. She desired her to marry and have a family of her own to which Shanta ingenuously said "No" because she had a greater mission in life than to just look after a family. Seeing her determination she was never forced for this again.

S. Shivdayal Singh and Kesar Devi's elder daughter, Kartar Kaur got married to Dr. Bakshi Ram, a surgeon posted in Sangrur. Their son was also learning medicine at Amritsar medical college at the time when Harbans Singh was studying for his Ayurvedic education. Harbans later got married to Bibi Ranjit Kaur, whose father was a *Granthi* at a Gurudwara at Lahore. Probably *SEWA* was in the genes of this 'Made for each other couple'.

Harbans Singh started his medical practice in Sangrur with a missionary zeal. In no time he earned the reverence of the people of Sangrur and the neighbouring areas because of his devotion and commitment to his work. He didn't just heal physically but emotionally and psychologically too. The icing on the cake was the temperament of his wife, who not only looked after the patients and the guests visiting them but would also provide them meals and hot drinks, garnished with her earnest smile.

The benevolent couple was blessed with a child, a healthy baby girl on 25 January 1942, whose name was to begin with the Punjabi alphabet 'E'. Many suggestions poured in and 'Inder Kaur' unanimously seemed everyone's favourite except for the mother, Ranjit Kaur, who was of the opinion that her daughter should not be named 'Inder Kaur' because *Indra Devta* as per her was not tough and strong enough. She would rather have her daughter named 'Inderjit' meaning the one who can conquer Inder. She believed right from day one that her daughter was meant to be *extraordinaire* and *exceptional*.

Inderjit was admitted in the primary school in 1948. The first words her father cited were, "Inderjit, enjoy as

Inderjit's mother – Ranjit Kaur

much as you want but not at the cost of your duty." And she made her father's words her lifestyle. Her work became her priority and she developed the habit of reading additional books related to history, religion and literature. She would wholly immerse herself in a book that she wouldn't have a clue if someone walked into her room and stood by her side.

Inderjit joined Government College for her matriculation. Apart from academics, she outshined in sports too, especially athletics. Reading was her hobby and even at a young age, she was well versed with the subjects of socialism, democracy, social security and capitalism. At the home front she remained gript in the household chores, aiding her mother and grandmother in cooking meals, scrubbing utensils and milking the cattle. Dignity of labour was another virtue her parents coveted her to imbibe.

Dr. Inderjit shared an incident from her young days that remains etched in her heart till date. As she walked down the memory lane, she ruminated, "It was an extremely cold night. The sky was a rolling blanket of clouds – the colour of wet ash, and the ground its dank reflection. In such a weather, a trembling patient came to my father's hospital, barefooted. My father looked at him with moist eyes and instantaneously gave him a warm blanket and a pair of shoes. The patient felt cosy and immediately dozed off on a wooden bench in the room. After a couple of hours, he got up and bowed down at my father's feet crying inconsolably. I sat there watching them and found it very inexplicable because there were tears in the eyes of my father too. It took me good three days to muster up the courage to ask my father, Dr. Harbans Singh, the reason behind their moist eyes. My father very lovingly replied that he cried because there were billions of such people around needing love and care and however hard he may try he would never be able to help them all. His tears were tears of 'Helplessness'. Inquisitive me, again questioned, 'But why did the patient cry then?' To which my father remained silent for a moment and then replied, 'His tears were a sign of gratitude'."

As I sat there talking to her, I realised that sometimes there are places and times that tug on our hearts in a strange sentimental and poignant way, bringing back to the surface that mix of emotions we've experienced sometime in the past. The symphony of such sweet moments is always so deliciously gratifying.

3. COLLEGE LIFE

In 1957, Inderjit cleared her matriculation with first division and joined F.SC. (Medical) at Ranbir Government College, Sangrur. At that time her five younger sisters and brothers were studying at different levels in school. Every time her friends from college visited her home, they were flabbergasted to see the number of relatives and patients already putting up at her place. The *chappatis* were being cooked on '*the Loh*' rather than '*the Tawa*' used in the normal household. All her peers were in awe of the warm ambience of Inderjit's home. On the other hand, when she visited her friends and the moment their families came to know that she was the daughter of Dr. Harbans Singh, the amount of affection they showered upon her was unmeasurable.

Although with time and age, the entire world was washed new for Dr. Inderjit Kaur…new pages of life… far away from Sangrur, in Amritsar today. Yet as she walked down the memory lane with a divine smile on her face, it seemed she wanted to turn the pages back and relive them. She shared yet another incident from her college days. "One fine morning, my grandmother came to my room, sat with me for a while and said 'Inderjit, look! You are the eldest of your brothers and sisters. You need to be a role model for them. I have full confidence in you and I am very sure you'll never do anything that may affect them in a negative way.' She said all that in a very calm voice. I looked straight into the eyes of my grandmother, held her hand and she pressed it gently. That was the moment when I silently promised her that I'll be a role model for my siblings just as my *biji* had been for us."

For many years, Dr. Harbans Singh had been receiving literature being published by Bhagat Puran Singh Ji of Pingalwara. Bhagat ji sensed an upcoming environmental crisis as early as 1928. He printed and distributed material for environmental preservation on recycled paper and created a movement against deforestation. Bhagat ji spent most of his time reading. He was highly impressed by certain writers in India and abroad. He generally picked up informative features from various newspapers and magazines and republished at his own expense and distributed amongst all free of cost.

Bhagat Puran Singh was born to Chibu Mal, a wealthy Hindu money-lender, and Mehtab Kaur, a young widow he was betrothed to in a '*chadar*' ceremony. From an early age, his mother taught Puran to treat all people with respect and to serve others. On her death bed, she made him promise to dedicate his entire life to service of others. He was to keep the promise, literally. Four years after his mother's death came the turning point in his life.

In 1934, Bhagat ji was handed over Piara, a young boy about four years old. A mute, mentally impaired and physically deformed, he was suffering from acute dysentery and was covered with flies and his own faeces. Bhagat ji brought him to the Gurudwara and cleaned him. From that day on, they were inseparable for the next 14 years (until 1948, when he assembled a group of those, discarded like Piara, with whom he could leave him for a few hours at a time). Puran Singh carried Piara on his back – literally – every day for those 14 years.

Puran Singh's inspiration to keep going was Piara – whose arms around him were the 'garland around his neck'! When the cataclysmic Partition of Punjab and India took place in 1947, Bhagat ji found himself on a caravan to Amritsar from Lahore. He decided to settle in Amritsar and start a home for destitute and the disabled. As word spread of an 'unkempt tall and thin man' who was caring for so many 'cripples', he started to receive donations. Donation boxes were set up around the city and the Darbar Sahib (Golden Temple, Amritsar). Slowly, he began to get small grants from organizations like the S.G.P.C. (the Shiromani Gurdwara Prabhandhak – 'management' – Committee) and from private donors as well. The inmates at Pingalwara received food, clothes and a bed to sleep in. They were also given literature that Bhagat ji had written or republished, because Pingalwara had its own printing press. The popularity and needs of Pingalwara were increasing and with the help of many contributors, it finally became a viable institution and got registered as 'All India Pingalwara Society' in 1957.

Inderjit completed her F.SC (Medical) in 1960 with second division and joined the L.S.M.F course in Ludhiana. She had heard a lot about Bhagat ji from her father. The literature from Pingalwara stacked up by her father's bedside, actually acted a bridge between Bhagat ji and Inderjit Kaur because the more she read about Bhagat ji's mission, the more she admired him and his foundation.

Once Inderjit read a very thought-provoking book by Albert Switzer in which he stated that he had observed that any and every living being fears death and wishes his life to continue. Probably that's why he made up his mind that he would do anything and everything to help each living being live a good decent life. Instantly she realised that Bhagat Puran Singh Ji was doing the same, providing each neglected person a life of dignity. Bhagat Ji, for her, was the Albert Switzer of Punjab.

Inderjit Kaur completed her L.S.M.F in 1965 and joined a condensed course of two years for her M.B.B.S at Rajendra Medical College, Patiala. Whenever she was back at Sangrur, she abetted her father in innumerable activities ranging from looking after his patients and spreading general awareness amongst local people about health and other issues.

As I am penning this emotional saga of compassion and empathy, I feel, my words fail me. I see so much more than can ever be explained and that sense of love and empathy just hits me in a nanosecond. I can feel my sensitive thoughts leap far beyond that which words can ever accomplish.

4. GOVERNMENT SERVICE

Dr. Inderjit Kaur completed her M.B.B.S in 1967 and got selected for a Government job. She was first posted at Barnala and her salary was Rs. 700. While at service, she remained busy the entire day – examining outdoor patients and looking after the already admitted ones. Dr. Inderjit has always been a person of exceptional gifts. She was like a bird in flight, making something so impossible for others appear easy and natural. At the hospital she calmed patients deemed 'difficult' by other members of the staff. She never hurt them, never became impatient or belittled their pains, physical or otherwise. She spoke to them like they were family, people who mattered, not just withered old bones too stubborn to die any faster. When her gaze fell on them it had the warmth of a daughter's eyes and her voice was deep yet honeyed. Her speech had a liberal dose of terms of endearment: with just her presence their pain medications worked better, their appetites improved and they slept more deeply. Dr. Inderjit was like an emotional morphine for her patients and they valued and revered her beyond words.

One fine day, she received the orders for her transfer to Sangrur, her hometown but her patients were immeasurably unhappy with that news. Many of the local residents tried their level best to cancel her transfer order because she was the reason behind their freshly established faith in the government's medical service. Once it was decided that there would be no change in the transfer order, a public farewell party was organised. It was for the very first time that a doctor of a government hospital was given a public farewell.

Dr. Inderjit Kaur returned to her hometown and joined the Family Planning department of the hospital in Sangrur. At that time, Dr. Ranjit Kaur was heading the Woman's wing of the hospital. She was the sister of two prominent doctors from Patiala – Dr. Amarjit Singh and Dr. Jagdish Singh. The most attention-grabbing fact about those doctor siblings was that their father was raised and brought up in an orphanage. His grit and fortitude helped him fight against all the odds and he ended up serving as a Magistrate at Patiala Courts. He raised his five children with devotion and they all joined the medical stream and became eminent doctors.

Dr. Ranjit Kaur used to address Inderjit's father as '*Bhraa ji/brother*' and her mother as '*Bhabhiji/sister-in-law*'. After Inderjit lost her father, Dr. Ranjit Kaur became her mentor and guide. A couple of weeks after Dr. Ranjit's transfer, a medical representative came over to see Dr. Inderjit and asked, "Has your mother been transferred?" To which she replied, "She is not my mother, but no less than my mother too."

It was during that period that Dr. Inderjit got to know more about Bhagat Puran Singh ji's life and ideology. Bhagat ji – who was every discarded, ostracised person's mother, who was unfortunate enough to be abandoned by his family but fortunate enough to fall into this man's lap who would become their mother. A man who sacrificed his personal life for the welfare of those who didn't have a life. Bhagat ji – an embodiment of compassion and selfless service.

Every time I pick up my pen to write about Bhagat Puran ji and Pingalwara, their mere mention evokes awe and respect. Leave alone emulating him, it is a daunting task to even imagine doing the kind of service he did for the disadvantaged and disenfranchised. Literature printed by Bhagat ji reached Inderjit's home through a fund collector. The more she read the literature the more she understood humanity and benevolence. Nobody could have imagined it back then that God was preparing young Inderjit to be the flag bearer of the Pingalwara in the years to come.

On one hand, Inderjit spent a major chunk of her day looking after her patients while on the other hand, with each passing day the concern of her mother and grandmother regarding her marriage appeared to intensify. One evening her grandmother called her over and asked her about her plans for marriage. Inderjit grinned and very graciously yet decisively answered back, "Marriage isn't my cup of tea. And I am very sure about it." The next morning her parents asked her the same question yet again to which she very gently replied, "When Florence Nightingale turned 30, her parents asked her the very same question what you all are asking me today to which she had replied – I am thirty now, the age when Christ began his mission. No more childish things, no more marriage discussions. Father, Mother, I am going to be a nurse." They say Nightingale's father was taken aback. In a fit of rage he again questioned, 'Have you gone insane or what?' To which Florence responded, 'You are right dad I truly have and I thank God for this insanity.' I too am grateful for this absurdity *Bhapaji*." Her father was well aware of his daughter's strength of mind. This issue was buried that very moment for good. To remain single was Inderjit's first independent and courageous decision that changed the course of her life. Just like Florence Nightingale, she too wanted to get away from this painted and powered artificiality. She wanted to come to grip with life, to know real people in their moments of suffering.

5. TOUGH TIMES DO NOT LAST, TOUGH PEOPLE DO

Inderjit's father was diagnosed with a heart ailment (myocardial infarction) and he being the only earning member, was immensely concerned about the financial condition of his family in the days to come. Probably that's why in 1974, the devoted daughter took the second independent decision of her life – resigning from government service. Although at that time, government doctors were being paid a handsome salary with additional perks too, yet in her case they were insufficient to sustain the expenses of her family. Moreover, she wanted to serve the society with a free mind without being tied down by any terms and clauses. Eventually she started working at her father's hospital.

Dr. Inderjit Kaur had no clue about the mysterious clouds hovering over their sky at that point of time. The lady she valued the most, her grandmother, passed away after a brief illness leaving every member of her family devastated. It was for the very first time that Inderjit felt the pain of losing someone close and that brutal reality called death, shook her from within.

As if that wasn't enough, in August 1975 Inderjit's father Dr. Harbans Singh, succumbed to a massive heart attack and passed away unexpectedly. He was 66 years old then.

When your father dies, say the Irish...
You lose your umbrella against bad weather...

As I heard the tale, for a split-second I stepped into the shoes of the eldest daughter of Dr. Harbans Singh, Inderjit Kaur, I had goose bumps visualising the thought of losing a parent and I felt it like a hole in the gum when a tooth falls out. Every food can be chewed, eaten because there are many other teeth but the tongue keeps going back to that empty space, where all the nerves are raw.

For Dr. Harban's family, the feeling of bereavement was so intense that it was virtually unbearable. For young Inderjit losing her father precipitously seemed agonisingly cavernous. The news of the death had spread like wild fire in the entire city. Thousands gathered at the cremation ground to bid adieu to the most benevolent person of the community.

Joginder Singh, the fund collector from Pingalwara, was requested to notify Bhagat ji about the demise of Dr. Harbans Singh. The 32-year-old daughter of the great humanitarian, Inderjit, felt lost in the chaotic enormous world without her father. She felt incomplete and disarrayed. She believed her family needed a shielding, fatherly figure like Bhagat Puran Singh ji in their lives to help them stay on the righteous path. Inderjit's cousin, Dr. Anand Singh, especially went all the way to Amritsar to request Bhagat ji to attend the *bhog* ceremony of the departed soul. And he did. Bhagat ji came and stayed with the family for a couple of days. He was in a rush the day he had to leave back for Amritsar. They hired a *rickshaw* and Inderjit accompanied Bhagat ji to the railway station. On the way to the station, Bhagat ji saw a nail lying in the middle of the road and because he was running late, he did not have enough time in his hands to stop and clear the road. They reached the station and before boarding the train, very gently, Bhagat ji urged, "Bibiji, there is a nail lying in the middle of the road. On the way back, kindly pick it up otherwise it's going to hurt me even in Amritsar." He then shut his eyes and as he slipped into a meditative mode, he again said, "My mother might get hurt if she walks down that road." (Bhagat ji's mother had left for the heavenly abode in 1930.) That was the day Inderjit realised that Bhagat ji saw his mother in every female around him.

6. THE SPIRITUAL BOND

BHAGAT PURAN SINGH JI
1904 - 1992
Founder Pingalwara, Amritsar

Bhagat Puran ji was extremely sensitive and highly expressive. He was well versed with the art of letter writing. He wrote a lengthy, poignant letter to Inderjit when he went back to Amritsar after attending the *bhog* ceremony of her father. Inderjit unfortunately misplaced that letter but she had read it innumerable times so the words remain incised on her soul and heart. He had written, "I crossed the threshold of your home with the same fear that someone carries in his heart while he does the *parikarma of Shri Darbar Sahib*. I could sense the vibes of divinity that envelope your abode the very moment I stepped in and I was immeasurably glad seeing your conviction in *Gurbani*. The warmth and affection that you and your siblings sprinkled on me makes me believe that I am no longer a person who is deprived of a family. So from this point onwards, I rightfully take myself as the head of your family who will always be your rooftop to shield you all against the scorching sun and the horrendous winter." This letter became a adhesive that cemented the pious spiritual bond between Bhagat ji and Bibi Inderjit Kaur.

If on one hand, the Almighty had been unfair to take away Inderjit's biological father while on the other, He up there was generous enough to allow a virtuous and saintly figure like Bhagat Puran ji to be the guiding light in their otherwise gloomy lives. Dr. Inderjit cited, "That was the chapter of my life when I was sad and happy at the same time. There were times when I found myself fully immersed in pessimism trying hard to find answers to a few 'whys', yet at other times I was brimming with gratitude, love and assurance. At times when the pang of separation from my father became unbearable, I would catch the bus from Sangrur to Ludhiana and from there, I would board the train to Amritsar. I would touch

Pingalwara by one in the afternoon and spend four hours with Bhagat ji before leaving back for Sangrur at five in the evening. In those four hours, Bhagat ji tried to drill in me all the knowledge and compassion he possessed, with an aim to transform me into a better and kinder human being."

Even though he gave his entire life looking after the pained, dejected and neglected yet he expected nothing in return from anybody. Many a times he would open his heart before Inderjit and often say, "*Mera kehra koi hai…mein te sarkaan te rull ke marna hai…*" Also he was extremely petrified of paralytic stroke and would say, "*Je meinu adrang ho gaya….pher ki banega?*"

Dr. Inderjit and her siblings were indebted that Bhagat Puran ji opted to be the head of their family. She fondly recalled an incident when her younger sister Preet had just moved into her newly constructed home. Preet could not contain her exhilaration and invited Babaji to her new abode. Bhagat ji didn't seem too delighted with the colossal building and said, "*Eney kamreyaa di ki lor si? Do kamre paune sann, baaki rukh lagaune sann. Banaun ton pehla mere kolon naksha kyo nai paas karaya?*" Preet was dumbfounded for a while hearing Bhagat ji's comments. She sheepishly said, "*Mein te chaain chaain lai ke aayi si per jhirkaan hi pai gaiyaan.*" But those *Jhirkaan* was nothing else but unconditional love for Preet and her family.

7. DAYAA SINGH

Bhagat Puran was a visionary, a sagacious soul who was overly apprehensive about Pingalwara's future after him. Pingalwara was the result of his sweat and blood. Just like a gardener who handles and nurtures his plants with paramount caution and care and is exceedingly jubilant seeing them bloom, Bhagat ji too was happy seeing his 'Home of the Homeless' surpass gender, community and religion and grow into a Temple of Humanity. He wanted to hand over the reins of this invaluable mission of his in the hands of someone compassionate and considerate. In 1975, a very good looking, bonny child became a part of Pingalwara. Bhagat ji named him 'Dayaa Singh' and wanted somebody extremely empathetic to raise him. Bhagat ji tried spending a lot of quality time with him. Bibi Inderjit recollected an incident when she went to see Bhagat ji once and he familiarized and introduced Dayaa Singh to her. He said, "*Mere maran ton magro tu hi is bache di parwarish kerni hai. Es nu wadda ho ke tera pariwaar opraa naa lagey, es lai kadi eh ethe reha karega kade tuhade ghar. Mein chahunda haan ke mere marann ton pehla eh bacha usey teebartaa naal, mere dil te dimaag de gunaa naal, meri paalnaa dwaara jeeon layi tiyaar ho janda jis teebrata naal mein jee reha haan. Te bibi ji, meinu eyon lagda hai k tu oh saare gunn rakhdi hain jehre mere jaisa puttar paalan layi kisi maa vich honey chahide hun.*" Dayaa Singh was always accompanied by Bibi Nirmala who was his caretaker, another assistant Ram ji and yet another Sewadaar Teja Singh.

Bhagat ji had made up his mind about Dayaa Singh by the time he turned ten. He had immense faith in Inderjit's mother and her ways of nurturing and educating children. After meeting kind-hearted Inderjit and her equally sensitive siblings, Bhagat ji was more than sure that they had grown up to be sensitive humans because of their mother's rearing. So he sent Dayaa Singh to Sangrur to live with Inderjit and her family. In no time Dayaa became the apple of their eyes and the axle around which the entire family revolved. In 1976, when Inderjit lost her father and the entire family was drowned in grief, Dayaa Singh seemed godsend and proved to be a blessing. With the consent of Bhagat ji, Inderjit's younger sister renamed Dayaa Singh as 'Dayaajot Singh'. Each member of the family tried their level best to inculcate virtues and warmth in Dayaa's character. On his birthdays, Inderjit would take him to leprosy centre to distribute sweets and spend time with the patients there. Inderjit's mother would snuggle him and tell him bedtime stories about the Sikh Gurus and their valour. Bhagat Puran Singh was very particular about Dayaa's diet and anybody from their family who visited Pingalwara would have to answer Bhagat ji's endless questions about Dayaa Singh and his diet.

"Dayaa Singh kina dudh peenda hai? Dudh tuhade ghar kehra hunda hai? Majaan da yaa Gokaa? Agar gaan nai hai te khareed lo... Goka dudh naal dimaag tez hunda hai."

Bhagat Puran Singh ji had heaps of expectations from Dayaajot Singh. Even though Inderjit and her family tried their level best, Dayaa could not touch the acme of Bhagat ji's hope and faith. Even though he possesses many qualities yet he lacks the ability to be the true Sewadaar of Pingalwara. Probably, one day Bhagat ji's prayers and blessings for him might bring a transformation in his capability and capacity.

8. DR. HARBANS SINGH MEMORIAL HOSPITAL

Love is a bizarre emotion. People who are in love end up doing stuff which they would have otherwise found irrational. Dr. Harbans Singh showered ceaseless eternal love on his children. He often used to say, "How much we (parents) love our kids is beyond any child's imagination. Although I feel you'll get to experience this when you step into our shoes one day, as parents. *Naa*, I guess, even then you'll never be able to comprehend the perpetual boundless love our hearts hold for you all. My daughter, all I can say is – Come to us any time… For we are your shelter, your guardian, your forever home…always with an open door, the key always in your pocket, and a love that is always yours."

Inderjit was studying in the junior school when she got to know about her father's heart ailment. From then on, each time she visited the Gurdwara, her only prayer would be, "Babaji, make sure me and *Bhapaji* (my father) depart from this world together. It's impossible for me to live a single moment on this world without him."

Dr. Harbans Singh was an immensely gracious and noble soul who loved *Gurbani*. Inderjit's mother had once shared an incident with her daughter, "It was a windy night in the mid of summer season and all of a sudden it began pouring incessantly. The windows became the drums, the concrete floor converted to the cymbals and the sound of rain on the grass signalled like sound of soft maracas. The entire family used to sleep on the terrace back then and there was a room upstairs with *GURU GRANTH SAHIB JI*. There was chaos and commotion all around because of sudden showers. After fetching all the portable beds and beddings downstairs, your *Bhapaji* straightaway went to *Babaji's* room. He held *Babaji's rumaala* in his hands and repetitively recited the *shabad*, '*Palle mein teinde laagi*'. His tears had mingled with the rain drops and his gasping voice echoed in the whole house."

Death stalked her father with no mercy or kindness. The hooded veil of death ripped away a part of Inderjit, a part she loved the most and she wondered as to why 'The One up there' did not notice her prayers of leaving the world hand in hand with her father. The very next moment a thought crossed her mind, "I guess the Almighty has some grander plans for me, some gallant mission to fulfil. Probably that's why He heard my desire but refused to grant me my wish." Today after giving a major chunk of her life to the service of humanity, the Pingalwara, Bibi Inderjit Kaur has surrendered completely before God's will. "Although I can comprehend His plans today, back then it didn't make any sense to me," she said. "And I kept on thinking ways to make my father's memory immortal," she added.

Inderjit was well aware that her father's prime aspiration and priority was to see his children do well in their lives. So she took over the responsibility of looking after her siblings and made sure they excelled in which ever career they chose for themselves. In the following years, her younger sister Rupinderjit Kaur completed her B.Ed after B.Sc and in no time got chosen for a government job. The third sister, Preet Inderjit Kaur, who was exceptionally strong-minded and hardworking cleared her LLB after a B.Sc degree and was posted as Assistant District Attorney with Punjab Government. She later married a bank manager from a very influential family of Kot Kapura. The fourth sister, Pritam Paul completed her M.B.B.S and desired to study M.S or M.D. but she too was appointed for a government job in Rajasthan. Her aunt, persuaded her to grab that opportunity and join the service. Later, she was selected for a job with UNICEF, a UN organisation concerned with the health of children. The youngest of all, Amritpal Kaur, very soon after clearing her B.Ed got selected for a central Government job and later married S. Gobind Singh Longowal, who got elected in the Punjab Legislative Assembly for two terms and remained Minister in the Akali Ministry from 1997-2002.

Inderjit became the task master and the mission maker for her siblings. She organized the chores and the academia like any good army drill sergeant. She tried living her father's dream by being the caretaker of her family yet she felt incomplete. She carried this secret desire to make her father's name eternal and his memory immortal. Well aware of her father's sympathetic temperament, the only possible way she could think of was to build a high quality hospital in his name, a compassionate place, truly a domicile of peace, care and brooding quietude. (A place similar to Miss. Brown Hospital in Ludhiana)

The land, where this dream hospital was to be erected had been purchased when Inderjit's father was alive. An extremely skilled architect, Mr. Lal, who had planned the layout of the Chandigarh Sector 16 Hospital was hired to design their hospital too. Inderjit was so emotionally attached to this project that she would often say that building this hospital was her last and final desire and dream. She was well aware that with the hospital shall come additional responsibilities too. She was very clear that the hospital that was being constructed in her father's name and memory would be an embodiment of selfless service and not 'commercialised care'. She pledged never to be an abortionist and till date she takes pride in the fact that she kept her promise. Dr. Harbans Singh Memorial Hospital was supposed to work on her father's principle and wish to treat the underprivileged people and the ones from the leprosy ashram free of cost. Probably that's why it took around a decade to set up this prototypical place of service.

The foundation stone of the hospital was laid by five special people – Inderjit's mother, Sant Harchand Singh Longowal, Dayaajot Singh(in place of Bhagat ji), Shri Wastav (the truthful deputy commissioner serving at Sangrur then) and the better half of her father's teacher. Bhagat ji was stuck up somewhere so he couldn't make it then.

In 1985, Dr. Harbans Singh Memorial Hospital was inaugurated with the *Bhog of Shri Akhand paath*. *Babaji's beerh* was brought in the room which was to be the operation theatre later. The white halo seemed to be beaming from her father's picture on the central altar. The fragrance of incense was heavy and the sound of Sant Harchand Singh's mesmerizing voice singing *Kirtan* could be heard from a distance. The spiritual journey was about to begin and Inderjit too was slowly experiencing her consciousness retreating into the abyss of her subconscious mind. This was not a world of fantasy, everything she could see around her was so real, so material, so substantial and yet so impenetrable. The atmosphere was brimming with gratitude and especially for Inderjit, the hospital building seemed sacred because it was cloaked with holiness and optimism. The hospital was inaugurated by Dr. Ranjit Kaur in the presence and with the blessings of Bhagat Puran Singh ji. But today, Dr. Inderjit feels that her siblings haven't been considerate enough in context to her feelings for this hospital. They took that place as mere property/asset, not understanding that for her, it was her place of worship.

9. THE SAGE OF PINGALWARA

Bhagat ji was diagnosed with a problem of prostate glands and hence was admitted to the general ward of Guru Teg Bahadur Hospital. One of the *sewadaars* from Pingalwara informed Dr. Inderjit about Bhagat ji's impending prostrate surgery. In no time she was by Bhagat ji's side. He seemed spry and bored yet beamed as Inderjit entered. His smile extended to his eyes, twinkling like he was greeting a beloved daughter. Where on one hand he seemed a bit solaced and gladdened by Inderjit's presence, on the other hand he was overly anxious and concerned about all his children at Pingalwara. In his mind, Bhagat ji had painted a picture and was extremely sure that he wouldn't be able to come out of the operation theatre alive. Nervously he continually mumbled, *"Mein bachna nai hai...mere ton magro mere bacheyaa da ki banega?"*

Dr. Sethi, the head of the surgery department, successfully operated Bhagat Ji but his body was frail and feeble, his hands shaking gently as he reached for other things. That's for the very first time when Inderjit realised how vulnerable he was and how much of a toll the sickness had taken. She had planned to return to Sangrur soon after Bhagat ji's surgery but she could not gather the guts to leave him at the mercy of the staff and other ignorant attendants. She felt that the rock who stood by hundreds of uncared and unloved deserved all the reverence and attention of the world.

Bhagat ji and Bibi Inderjit Kaur had the kind of bond a civilization could be fabricated on, just by following their example. Bhagat ji was a true hero for Inderjit – without any super strength or laser eyes and without the super power to read minds or move things without touching them, he saved hundreds from darkness, alone and so bravely.

Post-surgery, some complications developed which hit Bhagat ji psychologically the most. He was unable to sit or walk, consumed literally nothing in his diet, and to top it all, he was distressed. It took him weeks to come out of this malicious web of depression. Although he felt better emotionally and mentally, physically he still was very feeble. When he was discharged from the hospital, Inderjit took him along to Sangrur. He stayed with the family for a few days. It was Diwali morning when Inderjit told him, "*Mere kolon nai jaa huna babaji... mein tuhanu ikaleyaa Amritsar bhej dini aa.*" Bhagat ji's reply in English shook her from within. He said, "I will prefer to die in your presence rather than being treated alone in Amritsar."

Inderjit till date feels, "Ever since I can recall, I have always taken care of everybody around me. I have put my heart and soul into the service of humanity but the amount of multiplied affection, admiration and trust that Bhagat ji showered upon me is way beyond words and expressions. He wrote umpteen letters to me and today when I hold his letter in my hand, I visualize Bhagat ji seated at a table, writing, perhaps with a smile on his lips and sometimes a frown splitting the brow. His letters speak a lot about his frame of mind, his thought process. The smudges on the sheet of paper tell their own stories, blotches where once in a while a tear might have fallen. I have his letters wrapped up and saved as my most precious asset. Occasionally, I unwrap them when I feel low and confused and breathe Bhagat ji's words, knowing that the feeling of belief and trust for me and my work when he wrote those words might still be scattered on them."

When Bhagat Puran ji's health recuperated, he started addressing Bibi Inderjit as '*MAA*', and would often say, "It's only a mother's affection and care which is unconditional." Inderjit wasn't too pleased with this reasoning and would always revert back, "No Bhagat ji, a daughter's love is equally absolute. I find the warmth missing when you address me as *maa*. Please do not take away the right of being your daughter by calling me your mother." And from that day onwards, Bhagat Puran ji never addressed Inderjit as '*Maa*'.

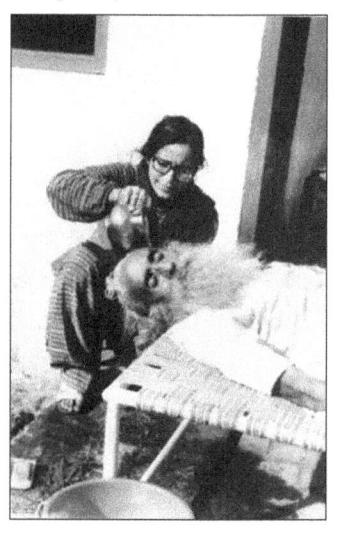

Bhagat ji was well aware that money controlled the world and emotions stood isolated and unattended in one besmirched corner. That's why he would often say, "*Je meinu adrang ho gayaa te pher ki banoo...eh sewadaar te bibi, meinu bimaari vich vi paani da glass nai dinde jinaa chir mein ehna nu sau rupaya naa devan. Mera kehra koi hai, mein te sarkaan te hi rull ke marna hai...*" Probably that was the reason that he gave heaps of importance to Inderjit's self-effacing service. Bhagat ji had painted that image in his mind that it was Inderjit's selfless care that helped him escape from the horrendous clutches of death. Somewhere deep down in his heart, he was confident that the only person who had the ability and sensitivity to carry forward the legacy of Pingalwara, was Inderjit. Her name as the flag bearer of his Temple of Humanity cropped up in his mind but he kept it to himself.

On the other hand, Inderjit's sisters had been married off and her younger brother, Mandeep was in final year M.B.B.S. Inderjit was a very modest person with an extremely simple way of living. Therefore, whatever she earned she handed over to her mother and it was then she who looked after the needs of the entire family.

By the end of 1983, Amritsar became the hub of turbulence and unrest. Pugnaciousness was at its peak and every day one would hear stories of assassinations and loots, in and around the city. Bhagat Puran ji unwaveringly stuck to his routine of collecting donations for Pingalwara and distributing useful literature to the public. The only change was that he desired Dr. Inderjit Kaur to offer a handsome chunk of her time to Pingalwara, which was immensely challenging for her because of her commitment towards her patients and her family. Moreover, Dr. Harbans Singh Memorial Hospital was their only source of income.

The Army action at Amritsar in 1984, slayed countless people, including innocent ones. There was wrath and rage in the public against the government for this action. After a few days, a congregation of a large number of people was held at the gurudwara in Sangrur. 15 people, including Dr. Inderjit shared their views with the people present there. She spoke about how the Almighty reprimands and warns His people when they tend to go astray and probably that's what Operation Blue Star was all about. There was nothing rabble-rousing and provocative in her speech and in the words of the rest of the 14 speakers. Yet all of them were detained, including a blind person Bhai Isher Singh. Dr. Inderjit was the only female amongst the 15 arrested.

In 1986, Dr. Inderjit was entrusted a chore by Bhagat Puran Ji to visit the various wards of Pingalwara and handover a written report. By that year Bhagat ji had started addressing Inderjit as '*Bibi*'. She did as instructed and in no time, the written report was in Bhagat ji's hands. Bibi Inderjit's approach was very optimistic and instead of emphasising the lacks and paucities, she proposed certain changes to improve the situation. Bhagat ji was possibly testing her capability and concern in the matters of Pingalwara. He skimmed and scanned the report analytically and closely observed the remarks by Bibi Inderjit. He felt it was time to bare his soul and share his plans of handing over the bridles of Pingalwara to her resilient and spirited hands. Albeit Inderjit wasn't ready for this colossal responsibility. After the death of her father, the path she wanted to tread upon was crystal clear – to serve at 'Dr. Harbans Singh Memorial Hospital' was not only her intention but objective of life. She was more than willing to offer her services to the Pingalwara but was reluctant to stay there permanently. Bhagat ji on the other hand was wholly immersed in the apprehensions and uncertainties that swamped Pingalwara and wouldn't take no for an answer. Gently he shoved the register before Inderjit for her signature. Inderjit carefully went through the reports recorded in the register. There was a resolution nominating her as the member of the Pingalwara Society. She was happy and gratified after signing knowing that it wasn't solely on her shoulders and she would be one of the seven members. In the year 1988, Bhagat ji passed a resolution in which Dr. Inderjit Kaur was elected as the vice president of the All India Pingalwara Society. After a while, Bhagat ji wrote his will nominating Inderjit as his successor. This was all done behind closed doors and Inderjit wasn't insinuated about it.

In June 1992, Bhagat ji got unwell because of intestine obstruction and was admitted to S. Waryam Singh Hospital instantaneously. Dr. Inderjit was informed by a *sewadaar* and she was there by his side in no time. Bhagat ji was operated and after a couple of days the then chief minister of Punjab, S. Beant Singh personally visited the hospital to enquire about his health and recovery. After spending some time with Bhagat ji, he clinched that the patient needed better care and treatment, so he instructed the administration to provide him a helicopter to shift him to PGI at Chandigarh. Undoubtedly, PGI offered better facilities and care. He was operated for the third time at PGI. A few hours after surgery, Bhagat ji slipped into coma and was on ventilator. Bibi Inderjit Kaur and Manjit Kaur Nurse were the only two people attending him in the ICU. On the 5th of August, the sage of Pingalwara passed away. The last few days of this servant of the hapless and the forlorn were full of pain which reminded one of the suffering of Christ on the cross. The day his passing into eternity was the sixth day of August. Pasternak says in, 'Zhivago's Poems', "You walked in a loose crowd...then someone remembered...that by the old calendar...today was the sixth of August....The Lord's Transfiguration." Was it a coincidence or a manifestation of the Supreme will?

Bhog ceremony was held on the 14th of August at Manji Sahab, Darbar Sahib. Bhagat Puran Singh ji's 'will' was read out publically, which pronounced Bibi Inderjit Kaur as his nominated successor. It was anticipated that she would stay in Amritsar for a few days after the *bhog* but to everyone's astonishment she returned to Sangrur the very next day. Inderjit was overly anxious about the patients at her hospital back home for she hadn't been able to attend them for the couple of months. She was convinced that Pingalwara affairs would continue to run pleasingly as they had in the past.

10. EH JANAM TUMHARE LEKHE

For the next four years, Bibi Inderjit Kaur visited Pingalwara once a week. Over the period of time few complaints had started surfacing which needed exigent action and correction. Torn currency notes were found in the donor boxes in Chandigarh and it was rightly predicted that someone had tried thieving them. Bibi Inderjit Kaur seemed dazed and shaken as she was well aware that such incidents could tremor the faith of the donors. Regret washed over her like the long slow waves on a shallow beach. Each wave was icy cold and sent shivers down her spine. This guilt of ignoring Pingalwara sat not on her chest but inside her brain. What if she was a failure and because of her negligence Bhagat ji's half a decade of selfless efforts went down the drain! And that very night when the guilt came again to haunt and terrify her, she took a deep breath and asked herself, "Sangrur hospital or Pingalwara?" The dawn came with a musical silence, the soul hearing the melody that the ears could not. A new day had arrived and on this fresh page Dr. Inderjit chose and wrote, 'Pingalwara' – the third independent and crucial decision of her life.

By 11 am, Bibi Inderjit touched Amritsar and called for a meeting of All India Pingalwara Society the very same evening. She regretted her choice of stepping into two boats simultaneously but she was back to amend all the wrongs. From that day onwards, service of the destitute became the mission of her life. Everything seemed peaceful on the surface when an unexpected storm hit her life. There was unrest and agitation within the premises, which was to sluggishly settle down in the next few weeks. Pingalwara had been anchorless for a while, hence the major challenge for Bibi Inderjit Kaur was to revert the impact of negative propaganda about Pingalwara. She was ready to cross any bridge to restore the lost faith of the people and to clear the obscurity of their doubts regarding the working of Pingalwara. With the passage of time, *the home for the homeless* started spreading its wings and 16 acres of land was purchased at Manawala where some additional wards were to be constructed. Ar. Mukhtar Singh prepared the architectural design of the different buildings of the campus. The days and nights of Bibiji gyrated around Pingalwara. She was so deeply immersed in the activities and management of the institution that she didn't even realise that her family had taken a back seat and she hardly had time to speak to her mother and her siblings.

Bibiji was amongst the first ones to observe the escalation in the number of mentally challenged children. Being from the medical fraternity, she was well aware that one of the reasons behind it was excessive use of chemicals in cultivation of crops and those chemicals were penetrating in air, water and soil, and ultimately in our food. Under her able guidance, a seminar was held at Mata Mehtab Kaur Hall,

Manawala branch of Pingalwara, to discuss and spread awareness on the subject 'Toxic Effects of Pesticides on Our Health'. She thought the best way to preach about organic and natural farming was to first adapt and try it at their own and so she converted their farm of 32 acres at village Dhirekot at Jandiala into an integrated organic farm including dairy, horticulture and crop raising. Within a span of two years the organic farm of Jandiala became a model farm as well as training and research centre for people interested in natural farming. The popularity of that farm rose to the extent that when the President of the United States, Mr. Barack Obama was to visit India in 2011, that farm was in his itinerary.

The Pingalwara has broadened and expanded its activities under the able leadership of Dr. Inderjit Kaur. It now meets challenges thrown up by AIDS and drug addiction, providing free education for poor and marginalized. Pingalwara has expanded through establishment of many new centres like Sangrur and Palsora. Dr. Inderjit Kaur's concern for handicapped, mentally challenged and deaf segment of society motivated her to establish a school for special education, a school for hearing impaired, prosthetic and physiotherapy centres for the patients in Pingalwara. She reaches out with a deep sense of compassion to the victims of several natural calamities and man-made disasters. Under her guidance, Pingalwara has rushed relief measures to different parts of the country affected by earthquake, floods, tsunami and various other natural calamities.

Dr. Inderjit Kaur has tremendous concern for environment issues, preservation of natural resources, prevention of deforestation, pollution control and natural farming. Periodically, awareness programmes through seminars and workshops are conducted to propagate these issues. Dr. Inderjit Kaur has received numerous honours, awards and distinctions in India and abroad for her contributions towards charities and social causes. These include the Mai Bhago Award by Punjab Govt., Panj Pani Award by Doordarshan Jalandhar, Bal Sahyog Award by Delhi Govt. and Bhagat Puran Singh Awards by Baba Farid Foundation, Faridkot & Punjabi Heritage Organization, Palatine, Chicago (USA). In the year 2006, she was presented Vibrant Indian Award by Developer India Foundation, Chennai. In the year 2008, she was awarded Sri Rama Award by Himalayan Institute Hospital Trust, Dehradun. In January 2008, she was awarded Padam Bhushan Award by Govt. of India. In July 2008, she was awarded 'Excellence Among Sikhs Trophy' by Sikh Council on Religion and Education (SCORE) USA and in December 2008, she was awarded National Minorities Rights Award by National Commission for Minorities. She was awarded 'Mata Khiwi Award' by Gurdwara Sahib Washington DC – Sep 2013, 'Life Time Service Award' by Sikh Religious Society Palatine and Punjabi Heritage Organization Chicago USA – 2013, Life Time Achievement Award by Sikh Directory London-2012. In the year 2004 she was invited to the Council for Parliament of World Religions Meet at Barcelona, Spain. In the year 2005 for her dedication towards suffering humanity, downtrodden and destitutes she was presented with a welcome address in the Canadian Parliament.

With that final period, I thought my work regarding the 'The epithet of compassion – Dr. Inderjit Kaur' was over, but as I was going through the final draft, I realised something important was missing. Even though Dr. Inderjit Kaur's life itself is exemplary but the fact is that Bibi ji did not choose this path with a desire that someday she would be placed upon a pedestal to be worshipped or would be bestowed with honours and accolades. Pingalwara was set up with the intent that no discrimination would ever be made on the grounds of religion or caste: its inmates include Hindus, Sikhs and Muslims. The biggest lesson to be learnt from Dr. Inderjit's life is to rise above religions, nationalities, castes and creeds and to be kind and compassionate towards one and all because they are necessities not luxuries and humanity would breathe its last if both, kindness and compassion evaporated from our planet...

Je Tu Labhna Oh Rangrez Nu, Ohda Pehla Rang Pyaar...
Tenu Roop Vatah Ke Parakh Da, Tera Jhalya Eh Dildaar...
Tere Hathon Paunda Kapre, Nahi Ta Baitha Vaal Khilaar...
Kade Bane Piyara Singh Ji, Te Tere Gall'h Da Banjaye Haar...

DR. KIRAN BEDI – THE ONE WOMAN ARMY

DR. KIRAN BEDI

1975

Once upon a time, a young, rebellious teenager finished high school and stepped into the girls' college in Jalandhar with dreams in her eyes. She got a chance to interact with young women from different social, economic and regional backgrounds. All her classmates seemed intellectually sound but lacked the courage of defining themselves devoid of societal colours. She was extremely disheartened to see that majority of the bright girls in college were there to study solely with an aim to attract a potential groom from a well-to-do family. During debates and other cultural activities, she tried explicating that education is way beyond a piece of paper which everyone referred to as a 'Degree'. It was something that made their gender audacious and courageous enough to voice their opinions and chase their dreams fearlessly. "*OH TU ZYAADA KIRAN BEDI NAA BANN...*" was what she got back time and again. The more her friends hit her with that sentence, the more she started idolizing the super cop and in no time Kiran Bedi – the Iron Lady became her (s)hero. She wanted to be like her, think like her, act like her... The first step towards 'Being Kiran Bedi' was opting for the subject the first female IPS officer had studied while at college. And what a proud moment for her when she graduated with an Honours degree in Political

Science. Little did she know then that destiny had its own different plans for her and although she would never be an unapologetically fearless cop like Kiran Bedi, yet she would be the chosen one to paint her (s)hero's portrait in words one day in her second book 'Overcome and Become'.

Dr. Bedi, the idol and inspiration for me and millions of girls around the globe, is the wonder woman of our times. Her identity is tangible and an aura brimming with positive energy always envelopes her. Her words are undeniable and her entire existence is immensely inspirational and unique. And guess what – from thrashing eve-teasers to winning accolades in academics, from gaining fame as a promising tennis player to being 'the first girl in Amritsar to ride a Luna moped', she has done it all. She likes her hair short because she doesn't like to spend too much time in front of the mirror. She listens to Jim Reeves but says she's not sentimental. Not anymore at least. She doesn't believe in crying. For her, control of emotion enables you to take positive action. An avid Wimbledon fan; Kiran even tipped Andrew Murray as the deserving winner ahead of his victory at the 2013 Wimbledon final. She enjoys a great relationship with her sisters, Shashi, who teaches philosophy in Canada; Rita, a London-based expert on autistic children and Anu, a San Francisco-based immigration expert.

The most admired woman in India, Dr. Kiran Bedi, has blazed new trails, discovered uncharted routes and responded to the call of her office in keeping with the letter and spirit of it. She has defied the system that had crippled and crushed her predecessors, probably because they weren't made of the same mettle as her. Courageous and charismatic, this is one woman who has lived life on her own terms. A woman can do anything, it is said. Well, here's one who has been a lecturer, a tennis champion, a debater, a police officer, a social activist, a television show host, a columnist, an author, an inspirational speaker, and an inspiration for both TV serials and even a film, *Tejaswani*. She lives life on her terms and seems to enjoy every moment of it.

Our (s)hero – Kiran Bedi, you are a gift to our gender, to our state, and to our country. Your first step into the forbidden territory opened gates for so many others. It is you who has given us the courage to chase our dreams, to 'Overcome and Become'. You always knew…didn't you, as to how badly the girls of Punjab needed a torchbearer like you…Our wings have already been bought…you paid for them…all we need now is to wear them and soar high…

Thank you, Dr. Kiran Bedi, for providing all the girls a platform to fly from, to inspect and to reflect. Your inspiring presence in our lives in the form of your actions and words is like the gentle nudge and the wise whisper.

2. THE BEGINNING

Kiran was born in a predominantly patriarchal joint family with paternal roots in Peshawar (now in Pakistan). The family later opted to settle in Amritsar. Her great-great grandfather, Lala Hargobind, a veritable Pathan, came to Amritsar from Peshawar. He set up a carpet manufacturing unit and a utensil factory in Amritsar and took both the businesses to great heights. He started off with Rs. 50,000 and during his lifetime, multiplied his assets with his hard work and dedication. His heirs were to benefit from that because he left behind enough property and wealth to enable the succeeding Peshawarias to grow and prosper.

As the genetic graph normally goes, Kiran's great grandfather, Lala Chajjumal, was a very simple and God-fearing man but her grandfather, Lala Muni Lal was something else again. At the age of 12, he dropped out of school and took private tuitions in English for about four years. He could relate more to his grandfather and his thought process than with his father. He borrowed 50,000 rupees from his grandfather to set up his business in the early years of twentieth century. His father, Lala Chajjumal successfully ran a wholesale cloth shop. Muni Lal opened his office above his father's cloth shop and corresponded with manufacturers in England in English that he had learnt so diligently. In no time he began importing the finest muslin cloth, the famous 926 *mulmul* from Manchester and grey and white Italian flannel from Bradford. He also purchased a dry, unused pond and constructed a *Dharmshala* over it, especially dedicating it to his God-loving and God-fearing father. Today, there are Peshawaria *Dharmshalas* in Haridwar, Vrindavan and Amritsar run by the family trust of Peshawarias.

Kiran Bedi's grandfather, Lala Muni Lal, was undeniably a self-made man but he was a headstrong patriarch too who held the control of his life and of all the others in his family, in his own hands (like a true monocratic). Kiran's father, Prakash Lal, was the third amongst the family of four sons and three daughters. Right from his young days, he had been a very keen tennis player and Dr. D.R. Puri (father of the famous sports commentator Dr. Narrotam Puri) who was the principal of Amritsar College, had offered Prakash admission and scholarship for his Bachelor of Arts on the basis of his ability to be one of the best tennis players. His father did not allow him though and insisted that he helped him at the factory. Prakash's elder brother, Manohar, had finished with his Bachelor of Commerce and would have been the right person to help their father but the two didn't get along well. Eventually, the dutiful and obedient younger son had to pay the price for it by giving up college to join his father in business.

Prakash was an extremely sensitive human who did not approve of the ways the women had to play a subservient role in the society, with virtually no rights or privileges. He was reluctant to add another submissive woman in their joint system under the tag of his wife. He made up his mind that he would not marry because he felt that his wife's condition would be no better than any other woman in the household. Prakash's paternal aunt (his father's sister) came back to live with her brother's family after her husband succumbed to death. She had given a word to a respectable family of Amritsar for the hand of their daughter to her nephew, Prakash. When he refused to budge from his stand of not getting married, she gave up eating food altogether. Finally, he had to give up and surrender to her wish.

At the age of 20, Prakash Lal married Janak, daughter of Lala Bishan Dass Arora, who belonged to an affluent and religious family of the city, who was known for providing charity meals to the needy and the homeless. At a very tender age of 14, Janak, who later changed her name to Prem Lata, earned the remarkable distinction of completing her matriculation with distinction in Ratan, Bhushan and Prabhakar degrees in Hindi. Her early marriage stalled her from pursuing her studies any further.

Shashi, the eldest of the Peshawaria sisters, was born on 31 December 1945. When Prakash held her in his arms for the first time, he silently pledged to himself that he would try to make his daughter all that he wished women to be. When Shashi turned five, she was admitted to the Sacred Heart Convent, run by an order of missionary nuns from Belgium. Lala Muni Lal was furious about the fact that his granddaughter had been admitted to a Christian school and that too, without his permission. Prakash was called for and asked to explain his action. He voiced his opinion confidently and said that his father had the right and say in the life of his own son but certainly not in the life of his son's daughter. For such imprudence and being such a headstrong, all his allowances were cut.

Prakash was aware that he didn't even have a graduate degree in his hand to survive on his own. He was trying to take the reins of his life in his own hands when his father-in-law offered him a substantial amount of money to start his own business. He opened a drapery store that prospered in no time. The partition and its after-effects however put an end to that venture.

On 9 June 1949, Prem Lata gave birth to another daughter who was named Kiran. The exigencies imposed by the respective families of both her parents along with their early marriage condensed the ambitions of her father and her mother. Their starved passions found their way genetically into their daughters. Thereby, Kiran inherited the genetic love for academics and sports from her parents.

3. BREAKING THE GLASS CEILING

The Peshawaria sisters studied at Sacred Heart Convent School, Amritsar, which was around sixteen kilometres from their home. Kiran's mother, Prem Lata, would be up at four every morning for the first chore of the day, which was to ensure that the cows were milked in her presence to avoid any adulteration. After an early breakfast, the girls would jog or walk around five kilometres to catch the bus to school. Sometimes the girls had to face the awkward moment at school when they had to explain in detail about the reason for late fees. "Shashi would do the explaining, as she was the eldest and in year seven. I must have been in year one or two then, so I was covered by her explanation. Even today, when I think of that explanation part, it creates a storm within me," Kiran recalls. It wasn't that the family was poor. It was just that the finances were controlled by a close-fisted autocratic grandfather. Probably that's why at a very early age,

Kiran developed that streak of determination when she promised herself that she would make sure that every penny invested on her by her parents would be optimally utilised and accounted for. From there on, out of sheer vengeance she plunged into whatever activity the school provided – be it tennis, debates, drama, athletics, use of library and NCC. From a very early age, she had made up her mind that not a single moment that came into her life because of her parent's hard earned money would go unrewarded.

As Kiran was all ready to step into year nine, she didn't seem too happy with the combination of subjects the school offered for year nine students. Maths wasn't her favourite subject and she wanted to take up sciences, which wasn't possible at Sacred Heart Convent School. She was instead offered a subject course called 'Household', where she would be taught how to budget home expenses and other skills that would help her be an efficient housewife. That was enough to scare away tomboyish Kiran and she started exploring possibilities outside her school. A private institution called Cambridge College offered her science with Hindi and promised to prepare her for class ten board exams. That idea of 'Double Promotion' fascinated Kiran and she took the first major decision of her life which eventually came out right because while her peers at her previous school cleared their ninth class, Kiran passed her board exams with flying colours.

Kiran joined the Government College for Women, Amritsar after her matriculation. Political Science and

NCC were the subjects that fascinated and influenced her the most. In fact, NCC gave her the first taste of '*Khakhi*'. She immensely respected her uniform and took great pains to keep it immaculately clean, starched and ironed. It wouldn't surprise anyone that very soon she became the platoon commander and was subsequently chosen to lead the annual day parade.

Right from her childhood days, Kiran was almost always on the run and as she stepped into college, she oscillated like a pendulum from classroom to tennis courts to library, not wasting a single minute of her precious time. Very rarely would she give herself a few minutes with her friends to enjoy a soft drink with her favourite samosa.

After her theory periods at college, Kiran rode back home on her bicycle to spend a few minutes with her mother. She would change into her NCC uniform and quickly rush back to college on her cycle. She could easily have carried her NCC uniform to college and changed there but then that would have deprived her from seeing her mother's serene face in the hot afternoons.

Kiran was absolutely sure that one day she would do something that was not expected from Indian women. What was supposed to fill in that empty space of 'something' wasn't clear to her, but that did not deter her from preparing herself. Kiran, as any other Indian girl in the 50's or 60's, was surrounded by people that blindly accepted stereotypes of gender, e.g. men belonged to the outer world and women to the household, men as carriers for lineage and women as burden, men as policymakers and women as acquirers and admirers of gold and other jewellery. Kiran did not have to go to any school to learn that. Her own household practiced these norms – her grandfather was a typical autocrat whose authority and word was final and her grandmother was a lover and hoarder of gold and other ornaments. Kiran's parents were exceptions in every possible sense of the word. For them their four daughters were never liabilities and spending on their education was their priority rather than saving money and jewellery for their marriages. They provided all their daughters ample opportunities of education, sports and other activities so that they could carve their own identities and grow up to be responsible and capable individuals. From a very young age, Kiran was conscious and indebted for the fact that whatever her parents were doing for their daughters was unique and should be treasured and valued at any and every cost.

Besides excelling in academics, Kiran vigorously pursued tennis winning the inter-university title, national title and eventually the Asian title. She became the national junior champion at the age of sixteen, seven years after she was initiated into tennis by her father. She was a dark, emaciated kid who was sick and tired of shampooing her hair every day and of braiding and tying her hair in ponytail or tight plaits. So one day she just ran across to the barber's and made him chop it off to the style she sports till date: what she was told was called 'the Boy Cut'.

Kiran, as a girl, was more concerned with working hard at the targets she had set for herself than adding frills. She would often attend functions and weddings in her sports outfit because to go home and change would have meant sacrificing her precious time from her tennis and she wasn't in favour of that. Tennis improved her concentration and taught her indefatigability, endurance and tenacity.

4. TWISTS, TURNS AND MILESTONES

From a very early age, Kiran was determined to choose her life partner and to pay for her own wedding expenses. Her first serious relationship didn't turn out well. For one thing, she was strongly oriented while he wanted her career to be secondary to his. For another, her partner wanted a traditional marriage, including dowry and as she was not willing to be 'domesticated', she ended the relationship.

Soul companions – Kiran and Brij Bedi

And then as destiny had its plans – it was at the Amritsar tennis courts that the two – Brij Bedi and Kiran met. There was instant liking for each other, and within no time they decided to make their relationship eternal and everlasting. The two tied the proverbial knot in one of the simplest ceremonies that Amritsar has or ever will witness. On 9 March 1972, a few people including both set of parents and a handful of close friends went to Shiva Temple at 2 am and there the two garlanded each other. That was it – Kiran and Brij became a married couple. The very next morning after her wedding, Kiran went over to her parents' home to take her usual glass of milk from her mother's hand and then drive younger sister, Anu to school. She didn't want Anu to feel that Kiran's changed abode would in any way mean any change in her responsibilities. Three days later, at their reception, Kiran wore a sari for the first time ever. Looking at her reception picture, the first word that came to my mind was 'Personified Elegance'. It actually left me wondering that if Kiran looked so graceful, so feminine in a sari, why she didn't don the sari as her work dress too. To which she answered, "Let's put it this way that I haven't got used to it at all and dress, in my view, is a personal choice and reflection of an attitude."

As their careers claimed all their attention, both Brij and Kiran decided that they would allow each other to lead separate lives while remaining 'soul companions'. Before the two tied the knot, Kiran was serving as a lecturer in Political Science at Amritsar Khalsa College for Women. She taught there for two years, till she was selected for the IPS (Indian Police Service) in July 1972, the first woman to have made it. When she qualified in the police service, all hell broke loose in the Ministry of Internal Affairs. There was no place for women, which meant that she was going to work shoulder to shoulder with a very educated, egocentric world. They tried to dissuade her. At the interview, it was suggested to her not to go ahead with the career of police service as it was a domain predominantly for men, and she would find life very tough in that sector. Kiran threatened that she would go to the Supreme Court and that melted the resistance.

I personally feel that the Iron Lady, Kiran Bedi, is not the daughter of destiny but a product of her own decisions and her fortitude. Nothing in the world could sway her from her determination and goals and off she went to Mount Abu to the National Police Academy.

Once she was into the mainstream of her career, both Kiran and Brij realised that it would not be possible for either of them to make compromises with their work and so they decided to live their lives independently, with their souls entwined yet physically apart. Kiran's mother-in-law gave her tremendous support during that period as well as boundless love till the day she left the world physically (19 May 1994). After her death, Kiran brought her spectacles with her through which she used to see her with all her love and affection. Kiran's family support has been the biggest blessing as she often says. Her unconventional style of living was unique at that time and the gates of both the homes (parents and the parents-in-law) were always open for her. Her lifestyle broke new grounds for an Indian working woman. Kiran set new trends of living and working and set a completely new perspective of viewing things. Their daughter (Sukriti/Saina) was born in 1975, three years after Kiran began her career in Indian Police service. Shortly after her child's birth, Kiran prepared herself physically for another tennis competition and for her return to an active field assignment. "I was determined to live my life on my own terms. I had been brought up with a vision never to be dependent or get 'domesticated' but to fly high as I was willing to go. But alongside I wanted to share the joy, glory, and my happiness with all those whom I dearly loved, respected and cared for," she opined.

An urge to do something 'outstanding' made Kiran join the IPS. She was never once interested in taking up an ordinary job, rather was hungry for challenges and dares. One of the early highlights of Kiran's prolific career in the IPS was the Republic Day Parade of 25 January 1975 when it saw a woman officer for the first time leading a march past of the Delhi Police Contingent. The then Prime Minister, Mrs. Indira Gandhi was so impressed that she invited Kiran for breakfast with her the following morning. Her success encouraged other women to join the service.

On 5 November 1979, the Raj Path (the road leading from India Gate) staged an awe-inspiring drama. Hundreds of Akali workers in flowing *kurtas*, with cross belts holding empty scabbards and swords in hands, marched threateningly towards Rashtrapati Bhawan. As they neared their destination, their aggression mounted and with bloodcurdling war cries they broke into a run. Kiran soon reached the spot leading a squad of the Delhi Police to keep the demonstrators in tow. She screamed loudly on them to desist, instead they attacked the police party.

Kiran herself charged at the mob with just a baton in her hand and an oversized helmet on her head. Despite the continuous rain of blows on her, in an exemplary show of courage, she stood her ground till the demonstrators were cowed up by her sheer guts and determination. She was soon joined by her squad and the situation was brought under control. For that remarkable act of hers, Kiran Bedi was awarded the Police Medal of gallantry for personal bravery on 10 October 1980.

The following year, Kiran was posted as the DCP (Traffic) in Oct 1981 at Delhi and instantly she signalled the department the kind of officer she was. Delhi traffic then was chaotic and haphazard with construction activities going on all over the city to add to the mess. In order to meet the rigorous demands of her job, she would be up at 5 am and settle down for her office work from 6 to 7 am. By 8 am she would be making her rounds on roads in her white ambassador car that she had fitted with a loudspeaker. A woman's voice over the loudspeaker on the roads of Delhi left an impression on the motorists that a male voice couldn't and didn't. It was her command that the offending vehicles would no longer be *challaned* but would be 'spot fined'. The haves and affluent people of the Delhi society always carried the 'Do whatever you want' attitude towards the police and spot fining was a different game altogether. No amount of influence could help out there. Kiran made no compromises and granted no concessions. On 5 August 1982, when Prime Minister Indira Gandhi and her family members were away to the USA, a traffic sub-inspector, Nirmal Singh, found a white ambassador (DHI 1817) wrongly parked outside the Yusufzai Market, Connaught Circus in the heart of the city. Only after he had made a *challan* he realised that it was the Prime Minister's official car but wrong parking was illegal, whether it be by a commoner or VIP, he had been instructed by Kiran Bedi, DCP Traffic.

A lobby soon grew that resented her. And why wouldn't they! They were affluent with lots of pelf in the corridors of power and there she was, just a DCP and that too, a woman! She was posted to Goa, the moment the Asian Games being held at Delhi got over. Kiran reminisces, "Postings are a part of our job and they have to come sooner or later. I could easily have done nine months more. What did trouble me though was that my seven-year-old daughter was being treated for nephritis and needed me with her but no one was ready to listen to me. At that point, I realised that I had placed myself in a very vulnerable situation where those who had got offended by my 'arrogance of equal law' alone could help. I found them attempting to teach me my first lesson – 'favour' your seniors blindly, if you want 'favours'. It was very humiliating and repelling atmosphere in the corridors of bureaucracy. I couldn't bear it anymore. So I decided to leave for Goa, leaving my heart and soul behind in Delhi."

Very soon, the Goa Traffic squad, inspired by their new leader became an invigorated force. For the first time in years, the Goans saw traffic police in uniform constantly on roads and actually helping in untangling the snarls that were the order of the day for the Goa traffic.

The Exposition of St. Xavier's body used to be a momentous occasion for the Christian community of Goa. The body of the saint was preserved in a reasonably good condition and exhibited to the public in a glass case on the occasion of the Exposition. Thousands and thousands of people from all over the globe would flock to Goa on that occasion. The inflow of traffic from neighbouring state Karnataka would be almost nonstop. On that occasion, the scanty Goa Traffic Police would be bolstered by a few imports from the Karnataka Traffic Police. The purpose of that strengthening clearly was that the police ensured that the VIP cars reached the Cathedral gates. "The VIPs considered that privilege their right, the police their duty and the people their destiny."

Kiran, being the people's guardian, wasn't happy with the set up. She felt it was people's turn to avail their right of a safe, construction-free pedestrian passage and parking space with uniformed men to regulate the flow of traffic and pedestrians. The VIPs were given a nearby parking lot from where they would have to walk to the gate. But, of course, the public appreciated that gesture and the VIPs called for her apologies and explanations. One of the senior ministers of the Goa cabinet visited the cathedral. His car was stopped at the parking lot meant for the VIPs, and he was requested to walk the remaining few yards. The matter was reported to the then Chief Minister – Pratap Singh Rane.

Kiran was summoned to the CM's office and asked to tender an apology to the concerned minister. She replied, "*Is the honourable Minister not well, sir?*"

"*The minister has the honour to drive to the gate. You must correct your traffic arrangements.*"

"*You must be aware, sir, of the people's appreciation for the arrangement?*" Kiran had the courage to ask the CM.

"*Never mind the public, ministers must be allowed to drive right up to the gate,*" he insisted.

"*But that would mean no traffic arrangements at all.*"

"*Who made these arrangements?*"

"*I did, Sir.*"

"*Did the IGP (Inspector General of Police) approve of them?*"

"*Yes sir.*"

"*Then I shall speak to him. I shall tell him to change the arrangements.*"

"*You may do so, sir. But then may I request to be relieved of traffic duties.*"

"*We'll see about that,*" said the CM, ending the meeting.

The CM it appears, never spoke to the IG. The public was extremely appreciative, relieved and grateful but the ministers perhaps never forgave Kiran for treating them as equals.

The Goa episode though came into the limelight yet it wasn't the most talked about public scandal of Kiran's career. The first occurred in 1988 when one of her officers arrested and handcuffed a lawyer. Delhi lawyers alleged mistreatment and she refused to punish her officer and the Delhi lawyers demanded her dismissal. A group of lawyers paid Kiran's office a visit to discuss. The situation became violent. She was in and out of court for two years defending charges brought against her. Thousands of lawyers across India went on strike demanding her removal, bringing thousands of cases to a halt, crippling an already clogged legal system. Kiran refused to give in. Eventually, neither side compromised nor any side won.

5. TIHAR JAIL TO TIHAR ASHRAM

In no time, Kiran was again chosen for yet another 'punishment posting' and this time it was the Tihar Jail, where she stepped in unprepared. She did not know what to expect. All she knew was – she was in-charge and that thousands of men and women were incarcerated behind the rusty gates and high walls topped by barbed wires. It was 1 May 1993 and Kiran was the Inspector General of the infamous Tihar Jail, the largest prison complex in the Asia Pacific. She stepped out of her staff car and walked briskly towards her new office, which was a claustrophobic viewless room 20 by 15 feet whose bare walls and rats along with few other insects welcomed her. Nonetheless, in that office she called her first meeting with the senior staff, the DIGs and the superintendents of the four jails. The following Monday morning, Kiran went for the round of prison number 1, barely 50-foot walk from her office. The inmates looked shocked, bewildered and silent. She was taken aback by the blank stares all around her and had already begun to empathise with them. Perhaps, it was that empathy that prompted her to break the silence by asking, "*Do you pray?*" No one answered. She again repeated, "*I am asking you. Do you pray? Please tell me.*" She spoke in Hindi. She moved closer to the bunch and directed the question to one randomly chosen inmate. "*Yes, sometimes,*" he answered nodding his head. Kiran probed on, "*Would it be better if we say a prayer together? Would you like that?*" And then one meek voice hesitatingly said, "*Yes…*" and they all sang together – '*Aaye maalik tere bande hum… aaisey ho hamare karam…*'

Kiran's next stop was the women's ward. As she entered, all the women in the courtyard rushed towards her, uninhibited and happy, a total contrast to the men. She asked them, "*Do you read and write here?*"

"*No*"

"*Would you like to?*"

"*Yes*"

"*Very Good. We'll study here. Before you leave, you'll be literate.*"

Kiran's prayer with the men gave her the joy of seeing hope and acceptance but with the women, something deep within pulled her. She felt, 'chained and imprisoned'.

Tihar was nothing but a human warehouse where the inmates were living in an inhuman way. Some thoughts were continuously churning in Kiran's mind. What could she do? What could she ask them? She scrutinized Tihar Jail over the next few weeks. The system that she had inherited was totally derailed and the sordid reality was conveniently hidden behind the huge iron gates. The appalling muck and filth in the subhuman conditions inside the cells were camouflaged convincingly behind the make-believe façade of neatness restricted to the certain areas where the VIPs were taken around. The meals served to the inmates were doled out from round rusty iron containers. These containers were used for multipurpose activities like washing clothes, storing water, bathing, and even carrying dry garbage. Apart from being insipid, the food served was unhygienic as well. The barracks for the inmates were like torture cells with extremely poor ventilation. The exhaust fans were themselves exhausted, and the inmates knew exactly what the term 'roasting' meant. The summer months were agonizing for them all.

A majority of prisoners came from underprivileged backgrounds, and they brought with them a plethora of medical problems. Apart from common ailments resulting from obvious causes, such as malnutrition, unhealthy lifestyles, and cramped living conditions, avoidable maladies caused by alcoholism, heavy smoking and drug abuse flourished. The single doctor on duty could not possibly cope with the hundreds of calls he received each night from all the four jails. All that he did was to send one common medicine to all the patients: Parmol, a cheaper form of paracetamol. It was Tihar's panacea for all ills – from fever to an upset stomach to something less recognizable... When Kiran Bedi took charge, literally half the prison population was addicted to tranquilizers.

Once Kiran had established trust with the inmates, she introduced an intelligence-gathering system – a mobile locked complaint box. The prisoners could share their grievances without fear of retribution. The very first day the box was full of more than 200 petitions. The inmates complained about food, hygiene, treatment by staff, corruption and gangster control. The first step Kiran took was separating the gangsters from the rest. Her parents always worried that the criminal world would target her. For Kiran too, it was scary...scary in the sense that she knew that if she didn't turn the prison around, her enemies in the department would love to see her fail: which meant 'they would win'. They had obviously sent her to Tihar to fix her or maybe in the hope that she might just disappear. She had no idea how to run a prison: she was a trained police officer. She herself had to struggle, and when she went through the manuals of the prison, a single sentence conveyed loud and clear that the policy of the prison was set by the Inspector General and that was her. In an unprecedented move and using that discretionary power as the Inspector General, Kiran threw open the doors to the worldwide media. She used the media to highlight the prison issues and to appeal to volunteers in the community for rehabilitation programmes. In no time schools donated books, welfare groups offered yoga classes and approximately 500 educated inmates became teachers coaching the uneducated lot. Photographer Ajay Goyal remembers, "The moment you walked in, it felt like a massive university campus, definitely not a prison. The best part was that the moment Dr. Bedi uttered a word, it was instantly implemented. She also introduced the inmates to meditation as her motto was 'There's more to life than jail'."

The reforms were successful, but Kiran was searching for a program that would significantly help prisoners change their behaviour. "Because ultimately the inmates have to re-enter the society. Do we want to release a convicted murderer who has long been nursing revenge or do we want them to enter the society rehabilitated?" shared Kiran Bedi. She had heard about an ancient meditation technique called *Vipassana* that had been successfully used in the Rajasthan prison two decades earlier. She organised a Vipassana course for 1000 prisoners who would be required to meditate for twelve hours a day for ten days, in complete silence. The *Vipassana* teacher insisted there were no guards and guns. It was considered a grave security risk – mixing prisoners of different denominations. It wasn't that one such course would transform the mindset and lives of prisoners but the changes were noticeable and evident. There was less anger, less hatred and less revenge. In a couple of months the entire place was transformed, transparent, open and written about.

"Religious by nature," Kiran said, "my post as the head of Tihar Jail was an opportunity for me to focus on the kind of work closest to my heart – reaching out to people in dire need, understanding their needs, addressing them; providing an environment which initiates introspection, where they choose to look within without being told to do so." She succeeded beyond anyone's imagination. Combining her extraordinary power to make things happen with her fearlessness and love of human beings – "I feel like a mother to them," she said – Kiran Bedi with her magic wand of empathy transformed Tihar Jail into Tihar Ashram.

The place "looked more like an Indian village than a jail," said American nun Ven Max Mathews, a student of Lama Yeshe, who set up programs for women at Tihar. "It was beautiful, with lots of bushes and trees – there was nothing that would indicate at a glance that it was a prison. There was no feeling of threat or fear."

Though the officials feigned and pretended that they were very thrilled with the reforms at Tihar by Kiran Bedi but the underlying discomfort was very much apparent. A year later in 1994, President Clinton invited Kiran to attend the annual White House Prayer breakfast but she was ordered to turn down the invitation, which she did. The following year, she was again invited by the U.S. President. By the time she had won the (Asian Nobel Prize) the Magsaysay award for changing the prison into an ashram and because of that the officials couldn't say no. They were afraid of the media exposure. Probably, that's why they allowed her but didn't forgive her for having accepted such invites. It was nothing but human envy. In 1995, she was posted out of Tihar and the '*Anand Ashram*' became '*Anaath Ashram*' yet again. After Tihar, the department offered Kiran a routine desk job where she had no contact with the public. She lasted seven days and chose to take study leave to write a book about her time at the jail.

6. KIRAN – THE GUIDING LIGHT
KIRAN – THE AUTHOR

Years back, after finishing her graduation and while waiting for classes to begin at the university for her post-graduation, Kiran had three months of free time in her hand. Instead of spending that time relaxing at home, she cycled down to a school approximately 10 km from her home and would spend her entire day there with the kids teaching nursery rhymes to the tiny tots, making their learning playful and enjoyable.

Later, she went on to pursue her post-graduation at Chandigarh. Even before the results were declared she was offered the job of a lecturer at Government College by virtue of her being a topper in graduation. She taught Political Science to undergraduate students.

After nearly three decades in 1998, Kiran once again got an opportunity to prove her teaching skills. She became a trainer for men and women who joined the Delhi Police force. She added a new dimension to the Police training by not just planning and supervising the training but adding a novel technique – meditation to it. She conducted her training assignment at Police Training College for Delhi Police. It was for the first-ever time that a senior police officer of the rank of

Joint Commissioner had ever directly supervised any training. The Police Training College was situated at a place called Jharoda Kalan, which was approximately 49 kms away from her house. She not only commuted daily but also used the travel time very resourcefully – reading newspapers, magazines and finishing off all office work in the form of pending files. After reaching the college, Kiran monitored the quality of training, met students personally to get firsthand feedback and coordinated with her staff.

After Kiran took charge of the training, she immediately called the Police Commissioner, V.N. Singh and the Union Home Minister – L.K. Advani, to update them of serious inadequacies in the training of the police force. One of the glaring deficiencies was the absence of computers. Yet amazingly, students were being taught and trained about computers through drawings on blackboards and were even declared successful. The minister responded positively and immediately notified Kiran to meet him with the proposals. A few days later she took along single page proposals for computer laboratory, firing and driving simulators and multimedia audio and visuals distance learning system. The Home Minister thoroughly looked into the proposals and issued appropriate directions. Very soon Delhi Police Training College was equipped with the latest multimedia gadgets. And that wasn't all, just as she had done in Tihar Jail she introduced the Vipassana meditation program in the training college too. The main intention was to enable the staff members to take control of themselves first before teaching and policing someone else. A record of sorts was created in the annals of policing when 1100 police officers and trainees went through the course.

Another and probably the most important thing Kiran added in the structure was the feedback system. This practice was also somewhat similar to the petition box in Tihar. One locked box was placed in each of the classes for students to interact with the faculty and to also give their feedback on the quality of training. The keys of these boxes stayed with Kiran. They were opened every day and she was the first person to go through the feedback which was later placed before the staff members in the lunch meetings. Unanimously, Kiran and her faculty found ways to tackle the problems. Under her able guidance, the Police Training College took the shape of Gurukul, a centre of learning and spiritual enlightenment.

Kiran had secured the Jawahar Lal Nehru scholarship while she was working at Tihar. When back in Delhi Police, she saw nothing waiting for her. She decided to pick up a pen (using her Nehru fellowship) to bring out a book 'It's Always Possible'. She had all long preserved her work notes, especially those related to her stint at Tihar Jail, with meticulous care. In fact, her home library contains systematic documentation of records, which have been collected with great patience and diligence. This habit came from her father who would keep a regular record of her tennis clippings so that she could see them on her return after playing tennis matches all over the country.

After Tihar, Kiran was back home on study leave. Overnight her mother converted the living room into a study, inclusive of a bed to enable her daughter to work through odd hours. Kiran developed a personal style of writing. She wrote all day long and for as many days as the thoughts flowed. Once they stopped, she would travel (mostly to the prisons) to rip apart the mental stagnation and returned to writing with a fresh mind. Her Holiness, the Dalai Lama wrote the foreword of the book. It was released by Natwar Singh (former External Affairs Minister) on 25 September 1998.

Kiran also created her own work. She used the fifty thousand dollars awarded from the Asian Nobel Prize to establish a non-profit volunteer organization inside Delhi's most notorious slums – Yamuna slums. This slum houses a hundred thousand people, mostly rural migrants, searching for work. Bedi saw an opportunity to work in a major crime breeding area. It was also a place where she could operate without interference. Her first priority was to get children out of child labour and into schools. To keep them in a familiar environment, she set up schools in the alleyways of the slums with volunteer teachers. Parents worried that plans to educate their children would remove a major source of their income. Her organisation also provided vocational training to men and women to enable them to earn income from other sources, and very soon reached out to educate five thousand children.

7. IRREPARABLE LOSS

Entwined souls – Kiran and her mother

After a study leave of nearly two years, Kiran was posted back in field but outside Delhi. She was appointed as the Joint Commissioner (training) in Chandigarh. She was about to test herself as to how she would perform as the head of the Police force. And indeed, she was tested innumerable times in just 41 days (from 5 April 1999 till 15 May 1999) she spent as the Inspector General of Police Chandigarh, the shortest period of her career but the most traumatic one.

While Kiran was setting out to set right the Police system, she was all along doing so with a severe handicap. Her lifeline, her mother was battling for her life. After suffering a cerebral stroke, Kiran's mother was lying in coma at the Chandigarh Post Graduate Institute. Kiran's mother had travelled with her to Chandigarh. The mother-daughter duo shared an immensely loving relationship – almost an ideal one.

As far as Kiran could recall, she had never seen her mother sick and there she was resting in deep sleep. Their entire family thought that it would be worth it to take her back to Delhi. They thought that the change of atmosphere might work a miracle for she would be home again. Kiran sent a written request to the Government of India seeking a shift of Chandigarh on the ground that her mother was in a critical condition. Her request was granted by the Union Ministry of Home Affairs, and she handed over the charge.

Kiran, meanwhile, had rushed to Delhi to look for a mobile intensive care unit fitted within an ambulance which could bring her mother to Delhi from Chandigarh. The Escorts Heart Institute arranged for such an ambulance, and the family with the unconscious mother sped back, with the siren clearing the way, to Delhi. They went straight to the hospital praying for the miracle to happen but Kiran's mother never regained consciousness and died three days later. She had remained in coma for 41 days.

Kiran went back to Chandigarh to say the final prayers in the temple and the Gurudwara where the families of her police men were praying incessantly for the recovery of her mother. Kiran's mother had been hospitalized for 41 days. The prayers had been recited 41 times, and she too had been with Chandigarh Police for 41 days. Kiran shared in an interview, "Maybe if I hadn't accepted the Chandigarh posting, my mother would have been alive. She was so upset while leaving Delhi." Nevertheless, her next appointment returned her to the Delhi Police after 12 years' exile.

The umbilical cord between the mother-daughter duo still feels intact, endless, and unbroken. Kiran's letter to her mother speaks loud and clear of their bond.

From;
7, Kesari Baagh, Amritsar – 143001

Thank you Mother...

Mama, I miss you in every breath of my life. I know how much you loved me. You brought me into this tough world and prepared me to understand its challenges. You sacrificed and gave every moment of your life to us – we four sisters. Not once did we hear you insecure without sons...

Mama, you gave us the best nutrition always. You kept me healthy. You ensured we rested well. You taught us value of time because you valued it. You made us love education which is why all of us continue to be students and learners. I never saw you wasting time or merely gossiping. I saw you either at work for us or with us on the tennis ground or with daddy in the club when he would play tennis, billiards or chess and you played badminton. Mama, you taught us simplicity and value for money. I never saw you buy anything which was a waste. You rarely shopped for yourself. It is we girls who shopped for you and I know how much you loved whatever we bought for you. You felt so proud of your daughters whenever we got the right things for you.

Mama, I recall how happy you felt when I used to receive awards and make public speeches. How you ensured you be with me at all occasions. I too rarely went without you. I too loved to see you present. The people loved to meet my most beautiful mom. You were so beautiful...so soft...so caring... Mama, you always knew what I needed. You took all phone calls when you saw I needed to rest. Everything was so perfect because you were home. I returned home to you. You took care of your granddaughter as your own daughter. Never once did you say you were tired. You sent her to school, to play tennis, to the doctor when she was ailing and never disturbed me at work. It was because of you I could give my Police service all 24 hours. Mama, my service was your dream. You considered it as your own achievement.

Mama, I have only wish. That I come to you after I breathe my last here. I know you are in heaven and sending your blessings always. And Mama, if we are to be reborn we become the same home again...Same Daddy, same sisters and You Mama...

I cannot imagine growing up without you. I wouldn't be the same without you. Mama, I miss you always but I work for you, live for you. I want the whole world to know who my parents were. I wish every child gets a mother like you. I must have done some great deeds in my past to deserve you. The fact that I am still here is to do more, to deserve you more......

Your daughter,
Kiran

Kiran's feelings for her mother captured in the letter shook me from within. I feel at the time of such a great loss, a daughter's world is bound to give way to sights and sounds of horror. It is as if she was walking in the street and a truck ran her down – emotionally. The woman she loved the most was gone, but she herself was still here. And she repeatedly asks herself and the one up there, "How could that be?" The loss impacts every part of her being. Not only can she think straight, but her activities run on automation. To call it 'walking in a daze' doesn't approach the dark clouds that amass inside her skull. There is a mental tornado in there, which no-one can see nor comprehend. One may shut down for weeks, even months. But then, one day, the loss gravitates into new reality. She remembers all the good times, relives them, and moves on with her life. That horrible experience that she once felt had crushed her, enriches her and she comes out all the more stronger, just as Kiran Bedi.

8. UNITED NATIONS CALLING

Kiran was eventually promoted to the rank of Special Commissioner of Police in 2002. The promotion brought her closer to the ultimate responsibility: that of leading her 'favourite' Delhi Police as the Police Commissioner (although she was the third name on the ladder to police commissionership). One morning unexpectedly, Kiran received a call from the United Nations. They wanted to interview her for a three-year assignment based in New York. She had to compete with three other international candidates for the role of the police advisor, building civilian police forces in war-torn countries. Kiran earnestly prepared for the interview and went through it. Kiran opined, "I had been sabotaged through my entire career but that time was different. The stakes were extremely high. I was only three years away from my final posting of Delhi Police Commissioner. At that time, I was at number three in the Delhi Police hierarchy. The current commissioner and his successor were my worst enemies. I had been working under them for 60 days and after 90 days, they were supposed to write my performance appraisal. I was more than sure that it would be so bad that it would destroy me. So before 90 days, I wanted to be out of their control. The United Nations job offer was my only escape from them and believe me, every officer in the Indian police would love to end up at the UN. The only drawback of the UN was personal. But one can't have everything and there's always a cost."

Seven days until Kiran's Police Commissioner was due to write her 90-day report, she received a call from the United Nations about her being the unanimous choice for the post of the advisor. She was thrilled beyond words but the evening before she was to fly to the US, she was told by the Police Commissioner that her relieving orders were yet to be issued. She had to instantly inform the UN that she wouldn't be able to begin on the agreed date because without relieving orders she would be regarded as absent without leave. She decided to appeal directly to the Home Secretary. Her relieving orders came three days before the report was due. Kiran was selected to be 'The Cop of the World'. This posting was yet another first-time not just in India but across the world, and she became the first woman Police Advisor in the United Nations. She spent two years in the department of peacekeeping operations. During that time she travelled widely, read extensively, wrote regularly for various publications and interacted with various universities and institutions.

Kiran feels that one of the biggest rewards of the UN assignment was the surfacing of the missionary spirit in her daughter which was instilled in her by her spiritual companion Ruzbeh Barucha. Ruzbeh came to Mumbai to write a book and instead ended up shooting a documentary film titled 'Yamuna Gently Weeps'. Kiran Bedi's only daughter Saina and Ruzbeh got married on 13 April 2003 and are blessed with a baby girl named 'Meher'.

9. GOOD BYE KHAKHI

The date 25 July 2007 when India got its first woman President (Pratibha Devi Singh Patil), on the same day, Delhi – the capital of India too could have got its first woman police commissioner. But that wasn't supposed to be. Kiran was deprived of the ultimate responsibility as a certain coterie of bureaucrats along with the members of her own service sabotaged her return to Delhi Police, which was home to her. The coterie knew that she would go to any extent for changes, which they never wanted as they themselves never brought them about. How could they permit her to create an island of police reform in the country?

Kiran was firm in her mind and clearly indicated to the appointing 'controllers' that she would call it quits and put in her papers if she was overlooked despite her seniority and standing. She had put 35 long years in service marked by constant opposition. She had dared to persistently challenge the old order against all the odds. She had enough of repeated hearing, "If you cannot be a part of the system, why don't you just get out?" And she did. Life continued to be eventful even after she sought voluntary retirement from the police service. In fact, Bedi never looked back, almost immediately plunging into a plethora of activities, ranging from endorsing humanitarian causes to featuring in television shows and advertisements. In October 2010, Arvind Kejriwal invited Kiran to join him in exposing the CWG scam. She accepted the invitation, and by 2011, the two had allied with other activists, including Anna Hazare, to form India Against Corruption (IAC) group. Their campaign evolved into the 2011 Indian anti-corruption movement. Kiran split from IAC after a faction led by Arvind Kejriwal formed the Aam Aadmi Party (AAP) in 2012. During the 2014 General Elections, she publicly supported Narendra Modi, the prime ministerial candidate of BJP. Kejriwal, on the other hand, contested the election against Modi. After Modi won and became the Prime Minister of India, Bedi stated that she was ready to be BJP's CM candidate in Delhi, if such an offer was made to her. Eight months after Modi's election, she joined BJP in 2015. She was BJP's Chief Minister (CM) candidate for the 2015 assembly elections, in which Arvind Kejriwal was AAP's CM candidate. She lost the election from Krishna Nagar constituency to AAP candidate SK Bagga by a margin of 2277 votes, and AAP came to power again with an absolute majority after one year.

On 22 May 2016, Kiran was appointed as the Lieutenant Governor of Puducherry. This year on the 9th of June, she turned 70 and I am awestruck as I peeped into the routine of the vibrant, bubbly 70-year-old LG of Puducherry – a ninety-minute workout every morning, juggling between her stepper, having her tea and reading the newspapers. Breakfast comprising a banana, almonds and toast. Writing blogs, tweeting and lining up meetings. Planning surprise inspections at government offices, tweeting and scheduling public grievance sessions. That's Kiran Bedi, whose passion for her profession is not the only trait that sets her apart from others in the Corridors of Power. Age cannot wither her nor political pressure stale her infinite courage.

The office of this Governor, often described as a rubber stamp, has been anything but that. Kiran's critics may call her a maverick governor on a collision course with an elected government in the Union Territory, crossing the delicate constitutional Line of Control, but never has Raj Nivas or any Raj Bhavan been buzzing with activity of the magnitude (as it has been ever since Kiran took over), almost as if it is on steroids!

I kept wondering as to what makes Lt. Governor Kiran Bedi so different from most other holders of that high office? Breaking the 'palace intrigue' of a Raj Nivas, Kiran does not seem to believe in false airs or prestige of her office. Direct communication is her mantra. Conscious of her role rather than her position, Kiran is not the kind who hankers after the trappings of power or revels in cutting ribbons or lighting lamps at functions. The 'corridors of power' are meant to be 'corridors of service'. A little birdie inside Raj Nivas told me that she gets restless when there is no action! Weekends for her are not meant to kick up her heels and chill out but to hit the road with morning rounds.

I too have been a student of politics but all I remember about the office of a Governor is some basic information from my civics or constitution textbooks. But Lt. Governor Bedi has changed it all – youngsters are now doing internships at the Raj Nivas! Other Governors may have opened the gates of the Raj Bhavan to the public, Kiran has opened her heart as well and videos of kids sitting on her chair and posing for photographs with the Lt. Governor standing beside them, are any indication. Accessible to everyone with a problem or an idea, people seem to top her list of priorities. And like the proverbial mountain, if people are unable to meet her, she goes to their doorstep. The interaction at a home for the aged run by nuns is a touching reflection of Kiran's compassion.

Does the early riser also crash early? Not a chance. The Lt. Governor's aide Shivani reveals how Kiran would, after a frugal dinner of soup and toast, peep into her room even at 9.30 at night with some query or instruction to the social media team. A cup of hot chocolate before dozing off is perhaps her only indulgence. A workaholic can jolly well afford to be a chocoholic...

HUMAARI AMRITA

AMRITA SHERGIL –
THE FRIDA KAHLO OF INDIA

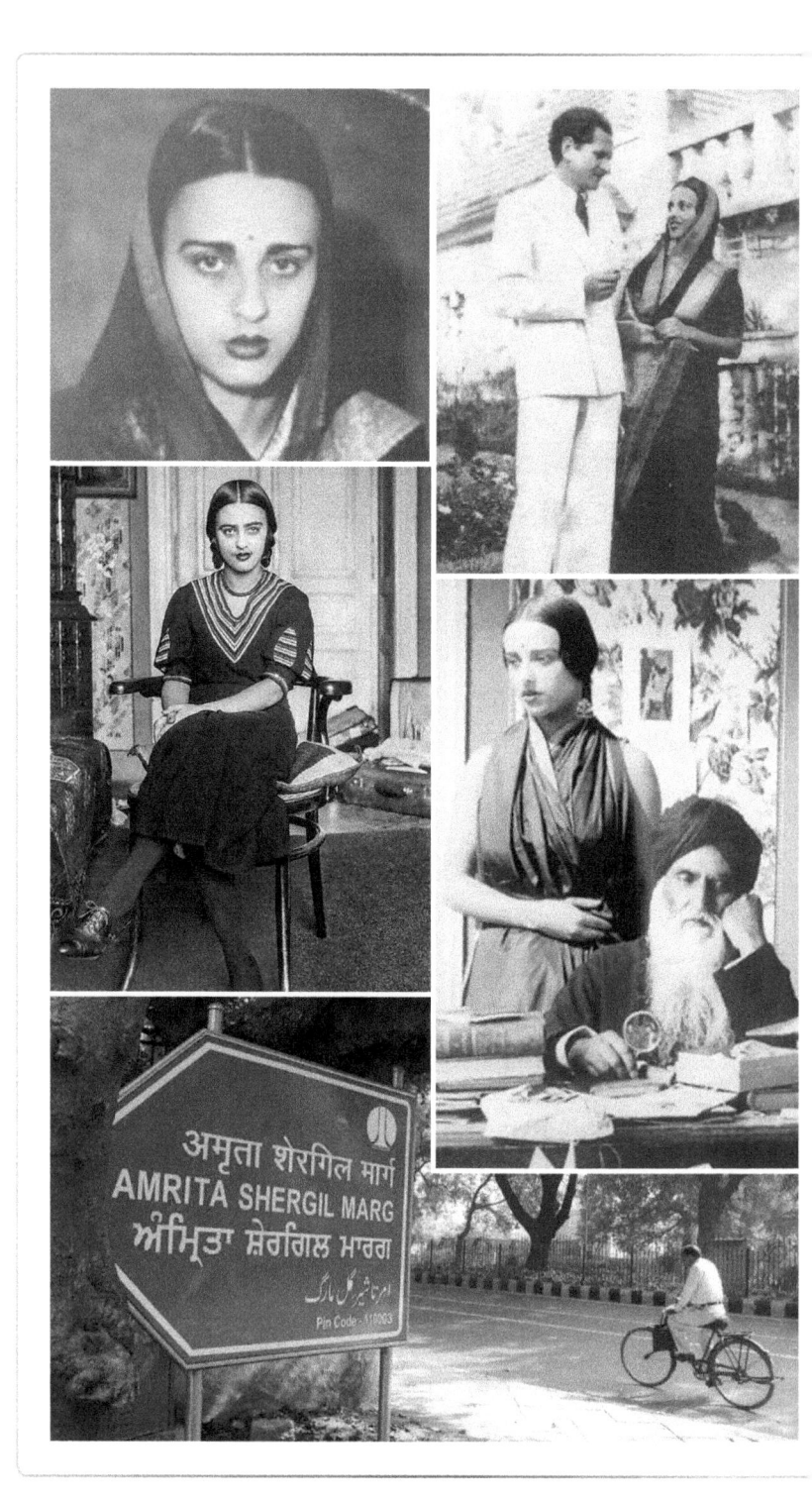

अमृता शेरगिल मार्ग
AMRITA SHERGIL MARG
ਅੰਮ੍ਰਿਤਾ ਸ਼ੇਰਗਿਲ ਮਾਰਗ
امرتا شیرگل مارگ
Pin Code - 110003

APRIL 1993

I first ran across Amrita Shergil's name while visiting a school friend in the early 1990s in Delhi. The friend lived on Amrita Shergil Marg, that posh little area just behind Khan Market in the heart of the city's elite quarter. I knew nothing of Shergil's work and was ignorant of the fact that she was one of India's foremost painters. I did find it intriguing, though, that in a part of Delhi where the streets memorialise emperors and other potentates, a woman's name was given great prominence. The name stayed with me, even if I knew nothing of its provenance.

Nov 2018

Last year on a pleasant Friday afternoon, I tagged along with my friend and in no time we were gliding across a colossal marble expanse of an art gallery. The gallery walls were carefully adorned with a constellation of artworks. Amidst all those extraordinary pieces of art, one particular painting became a crowd puller: The Little Girl in Blue (1934) (painted by the name that had been silently sitting in one corner of my mind and heart since 1993) which had resurfaced in the public realm after eight long decades. Painted in December 1934, when Amrita Shergil was just 21, the painting depicted the artist's eight-year-old neighbour, Lalit 'Babit' Kaur. Her mother, Lady Buta Singh, was a close friend who lived next door to Shergil's paternal uncle, Sunder Singh Majithia at Nowshera House. The painting sold for Rs 18.69 crore, shooting past its estimate of Rs 8.5 to Rs 12.5 crore, creating a record price for the artist in India.

The 'Little Girl in Blue' is otherwise known as Babette Singh Mann, a cheerful woman of 92, and one of the very few remaining people who would have personally known Amrita Shergil. She recalled sitting three to four times as her mother kept admonishing her not to fidget. She was likely chosen for her high cheekbones and a remarkable resemblance to Shergil. However, when faced with the finished portrait, Lady Buta was aghast because the painting did not look realistic enough and did not make Babette 'pretty' (i.e. fair-skinned) enough.

Shergil was said to have replied, "If you wanted a replica then you need a photographer." Shergil then told the family that she would re-use the canvas but instead she kept the work for her first solo exhibition in Lahore held three years later. However, to Babette and her family, they were convinced that the portrait was destroyed until she saw it again recently as it was publicised for the auction.

I returned from that art gallery with an unquenchable thirst to know everything about Amrita... The beautiful painter who never grew old, and is not just a National Treasure artist of India but also a pioneer of Modern Indian art with whose brilliance the world's fascination continues to grow. Everyone says that she is also one of Indian art's best enigma, whose short yet eventful life, and an even shorter yet prolific career, only add to the aura around her oeuvre that is truly seminal in understanding the growth of modern Indian art's own idiom. There exist few, if any comparisons in the history of art to Amrita. The influence she wielded in her tragically short life was enormous. With her avant-garde approach, not only in her technique and style but in her presentation of female subjects, she shaped the future art of India perhaps more than any other artist of the time. The insatiable greed to explore and share the adventurous inscrutable life's journey of this daughter of Punjab, Amrita Shergil, made me read every possible feature, write-up and book about her because I wanted to see, perceive and understand the real Amrita ......HUMAARI AMRITA......

2. THE TALE OF A PRINCESS

For someone whose life had been a step ahead of *extraordinaire*, it was apt that Amrita Shergil was born under a rather unusual set of circumstances – a Sikh father, a Hungarian mother, in the city of Budapest on a cold January morning. Amrita's father, Umrao Singh Shergil, was born in 1870 in Majithia near Amritsar. He spent his time studying Sanskrit, Persian and Urdu texts and was a scholar of philosophy. A nationalist, he was a close friend of the Urdu Poet, Mohammad Iqbal. In his later life, he came under the spell of Tolstoy, took to vegetarianism and became a teetotaller. Although Umrao Singh's education and interest rooted him in the Indian culture, he was always willing to bridge cultures and reacted positively to new, foreign and unknown. When he was very young, he was married off to Captain Gulab Singh Attari's daughter, and they were blessed with four children – Balram, Satyavan, Vivek and Sumair. His wife passed away at a young age, and Umrao Singh went off to London to complete his studies. It was there that he met Maharaja Ranjit Singh's granddaughter, Princess Bamba Sofia Jindan Dalip Singh, an accomplished young woman who was fond of music and was smitten by the handsome young aristocrat, Umrao Singh. She hoped to marry him but he fell under the spell of her talented Hungarian travelling companion, Marie Antoinette. Umrao Singh's attention was caught at a soiree when the gorgeous young woman with flaming red hair sang while playing the piano. Soon after they got married in Lahore as per the Sikh rites on 4 February 1912. Shortly after that they left for Budapest to spend time with her family.

Amrita's mother, Marie Antoinette Gottesmann, came from an affluent bourgeois family who were not only part of Budapest's upper strata but also had international connections. Marie was a brilliant pianist and singer and considered taking up opera singer as a profession and was sent to Rome to study further. Though she did not become a professional yet it is said that she had a well-trained voice and sang captivatingly. Amrita's mother was a vivacious woman with a flair for entertaining, so Amrita's family mingled with the high society of Budapest.

The building, 4 Szilagyi Dezso Square, was where the composer Bela Bartok had also stayed. Today, the house bears a plaque which announces that the painter Amrita Shergil, of Indo-Hungarian origin was born there on 30 January 1913. It is not certain that which apartment Umrao and Marie occupied, as no residents survive from that period – but the best description of its view lies in Marie's rapturous account of the birth of her daughter, Amrita...

"It is a Sunday, the bright, frost winter morning of the 30 January 1913. As one looks out from the windows, there is a lovely sight of dazzling glittering whiteness, a fairy scene indeed. Such was the day when Amrita came into the world. I can hear the benevolent voice of the dear old family doctor as he exclaimed, 'It's a little girl...and what a sweet one... God bless her!' A few minutes later the nurse brought me the little bundle wrapped in a soft, warm eider down... and I wept out of sheer happiness."

On seeing Amrita after her birth, her father wrote, "The most remarkable thing about her infancy seemed to me that she never screamed or cried as babies do. She watched things and people around her with large attentive eyes."

The things that she most looked forward to as a child were paint boxes, coloured pens and picture books. Rather independent in her spirit at that age, Amrita detested the idea of 'Colouring books', and always drew and painted herself.

Amrita was soon followed by a little sister – Indira and on 17 November 1918 both of them were baptized Roman Catholics. Amrita spent her childhood at Dunaharaszti playing in the garden or making drawings. It was at that family house that Amrita first became close to her cousins Viola and Victor Egan, the children of her mother's sister Blanka. Soon after, life took another turn and on 2 January 1921, Umrao Singh's family set sail after spending almost a decade in Hungary.

En route to India, the family made a brief stop at Paris to see operas, theatres and museums and Amrita was exposed to the treasures of the Louvre for the first time. After celebrating Amrita's eighth birthday on the ship, the family landed in Bombay in February. They soon left for Delhi and then for Lahore, where they stayed for two months with Umrao Singh's brother Sunder Singh Majithia. In April, the family shifted to their new home in Simla, which was to be called 'The Holme'. Marie set to work furnishing it with carpets, furniture and paintings in keeping with her elegant lifestyle. She also saw that her girls studied piano and violin along with drawing and painting. Amrita was at that young age a serious, introverted girl who read a lot and preferred the company of adults to those of her own age. She started taking art lessons from the artist, Hal Bevan Petman, a fashionable society painter who, although had recently left a teaching post at the Slade School of Art in London, seemed to have been best known for painting portraits of society women, and teaching art to children of affluent families. Amrita liked the atmosphere in the atelier and spent a considerable amount of time there.

At the school front, Amrita was admitted to a catholic school, the Convent of Jesus and Mary at Simla. Vehemently opposed to it from the beginning, she rebelled at the school's compulsory

Mass attendance – something her mother had never insisted on. She wrote a letter to her parents from the convent, strongly denouncing catholic rituals which she considered bigoted and narrow-minded. The mother Superior intercepted the letter and summarily expelled her from school. Amrita's formal education was over and it now suited her fine to spend her time playing the piano or sketching.

At the age of twelve, Amrita ruminated in her diary about a wedding she had attended in which the bride had been married off at the age of thirteen to a fifty-year-old man with three other wives. She wrote about the little bride looking forlorn amidst a roomful of ladies decked up in gorgeous robes and sporting the most fashionable gems and pearls. In the ambience of gaiety and festivity, young Amrita didn't fail to notice the expression of weariness in the girl's 'lovely, liquid eyes' and her silent countenance which symbolized her mute acceptance of the cruelty meted out by her parents and other relatives in whose hands she was just a 'helpless toy'. The empathy of Amrita for Indian women and their striving, often in the face of great odds, would emerge again and again in her paintings later on. The subject was always handled with great sensitivity and not with superficial pity and condescension.

Year 1927 proved to be an important year for fourteen-year-old Amrita in many ways. Her uncle Ervin Baktay came to visit them in Simla. He was a painter himself and had written several books on Indian culture and art. While in Simla, Ervin introduced

Amrita to some of the principles of the Nagybanya School of painting. He encouraged her to develop a sense of autonomy and to make careful observations of reality around her and then transfer that to her work. Later, she would say to her Uncle, "It's to you I owe my skill in drawing." Seeing Amrita's passion and skills, Ervin urged her parents to let her train in Paris, where she would have greater opportunities to develop her talent. The family decided thereby to move to Paris for a few years so that Amrita could study art there. This was quiet an unusual decision which not many Indian families would have taken back then. To move wholesale to another country for a daughter's education and that too in the field of art, was unheard of in the 1920's. Finally, the family sailed to Europe in 1929.

3. PARIS CALLING, INDIA YEARNING

"I can only paint in India. Europe belongs to Picasso, Matisse and Braque. India belongs to me."
– AMRITA *SHERGIL*

When Amrita reached Paris she was only sixteen. The city which was supposed to be her home for the next five years, was at that time the most influential cultural centre of the world, the Mecca of the world of art. The Shergils lived initially in the staid, respectable locality of Passy and then moved to 11 Rue De Bassano near the fashionable Champs Elysees. Those five years in Paris flourished Amrita's confidence and she became a vivacious and stimulating person, in full possession of herself spending her nights in animated conversation in dimly lit cafes. Her self-portrait in 1930, when she was seventeen, shows a brightly made-up woman with glowing cheeks and full red lips, wearing a low cut dress against a flaming red background. She seemed to be lured by the city's seductive ways, in which she participated like a voyeur, before distancing herself and watching like one dispossessed. The poor and the exploited, the beggar and harlot were objects of her compassion. Ironically, her distaste for the big city went hand in hand with the fact that she felt at home with it.

Amrita's studio in Paris was quite bare, a huge room with whitewashed walls and only a couple of Chinese paintings and the work of her friend, Marie Louise Chasseny, to adorn it. Alongside her drawings, she began to paint with oils for the first time and between 1930 and 1932, she produced over sixty paintings. While most of these were portraits and self-portraits, her painting *Young Girls* (1932) won her the Gold Medal from the Grand Salon in 1933 and she was appointed as the associate member of the institute. Amrita was delighted by the recognition, although she wrote in a letter to her cousin Victor that she found the atmosphere of the Salon very stuffy. But the prize would enable her to exhibit two paintings there every year, which for a student and a relative outsider was a coveted thing indeed.

Young Girls had two young women seated on chairs, in conversation with each other. Her sister Indira and a friend, Denise were the models. At times I wonder if the two girls in the painting represent facets of Amrita's own persona!

Then came Yusuf Ali Khan in the scene… with his handsome looks, dashing manners and affluent family. Amrita's mother, Marie Antoinette, felt he would be the perfect son-in-law. He was the son of Raja Nawab Ali, a wealthy noble from Akbarpur, in the United Provinces. Yusuf Khan happened to be in Paris at the time. Marie threw them together, inviting him to their soirees in Paris. Being young and impressionable and perhaps under some pressure from her mother, Amrita agreed to marry him and got engaged to him. Not only did it prove disastrous, for the two were very different and soon she found herself pregnant and had to turn to her cousin Victor, a medical student for an abortion. She was subjected to a great deal of mental agony. And it is from then on she decided to make her own decision about marriage. Perhaps, her disillusionment with her first relationship with a man spurred Amrita into the habit of forming fleeting liaisons with men, and that painful first encounter drew her closer to her first cousin, Victor Egan, with whom she seemed to have become increasingly involved around that time.

AA AB LAUT CHALIEN......

"As soon as I put my foot on Indian soil, my painting underwent a change not only in subject and spirit but in technique."

– Amrita Shergil

By the end of 1934, Amrita felt she had got what she wanted from Paris and should strike out on her own as a painter. She began to be haunted by the intense longing to return to India, feeling in some strange inexplicable way that there lay her destiny as a painter. One of her professors would often say to her, "Judging by the richness of your colouring, I feel that your artistic personality would find its true atmosphere in the colour and light of the East rather than the grey studios of the West."

Amrita with her father – Umrao Singh

Amrita's father felt that his bohemian daughter would invite disapproval from his circle back home and she felt extremely hurt that he preferred to conserve his good name rather than allow her to come back and live close to him. She tried explaining that she wasn't an immoral person in the true sense of the word and besides, 'Fools and mischief-makers will always talk, even if she doesn't give them food for it.' Although she longed for India, she acknowledged it was Paris which had given her a new orientation. She left the city in November 1934 and reached India sometime in December the same year. Arriving in India, she didn't go immediately to her parent's home in Simla, but stayed at her ancestral home, the palatial Majithia House, near Amritsar. Her first step towards pitching her tent in her home country was to discard all her western clothes. For the rest of the life, Amrita would wear gorgeous saris in rich, deep colours, chunky silver jewellery set with jade and turquoise stones and makeup that defined her dark, glowing eyes. It was during this time that she painted, *The Little Girl In Blue,* the painting which was sold for a whopping 18.69 crores in November 2018. In the advent of summer, Amrita joined her parents at Simla. Her studio was an annexe to her parent's house, The Holme, on Summer Hill and her living quarters were above it. The only ornamentations were a book shelf, Chinese paintings and a Javanese cloth over the fireplace. Amidst all that, Amrita painted and rediscovered herself in the verdant surroundings of the pine trees. Her first few paintings in Simla were of great sentimental variety – steeped in poverty yet aesthetically pleasing. And when someone asked her as to why she chose to depict only 'the sad and dark side' of Indian life through her pictures, she had confessed that she wanted to interpret the 'atrocious physiological misery' of the country which had impacted her profoundly. She wanted, she said, "to interpret the life of Indians, particularly the poor Indians pictorially: to depict their angular brown bodies, strangely beautiful in their ugliness, to reproduce the impression their sad eyes created in me."

4. AMRITA WEDS VICTOR

Amrita with Victor

Amrita and Victor Egan had been lovers since the time they were teenagers and she would visit Hungary during her vacations from Paris. They continued to remain in touch when she returned to India and at some point, of which there is no clear indication, they decided to seal their relationship by getting married. Her parents strongly opposed the union, particularly her mother, but this made Amrita all the more determined. The reasons for her mother's disapproval can only be guessed, but apart from consanguinity, for marriage between first cousins was strongly disapproved of then as now, she was highly ambitious and wanted Amrita to make a good match. Beautiful and widely admired, Amrita could, she felt, easily marry someone rich and famous and Victor was neither. Amrita, on the other hand, was sure she had chosen the right man – someone who understood and accepted her for who she was. To be loved for herself was something unique and she valued it. Moreover, she and Victor began their marriage with an unusual set of agreements. They would have no children, not because they were first cousins but because neither really wanted them. Amrita wanted to devote herself entirely to her work and Victor supported her.

Amrita and Victor married quietly, without champagne and roses, on 16 July 1938, a warm summer day. Victor gathered his few friends and they all went to the registrar's office, where he and Amrita completed the formalities of registration and were declared Man and Wife. Erno Gottesman, who was one of the official witnesses to the wedding, said, "It was a brief affair as neither of them believed in ceremony. There was no celebration after that." Although the wedding itself was devoid of the usual ceremonial trappings, the marriage was based on a sound footing, for the two were actually well matched. Amrita was idealistic and impractical, Victor was a realist and highly tolerant of Amrita's needs. It was a pleasant trusting relationship because they knew each other so well.

The two love birds – Amrita and Victor

After their marriage, the two reached Simla, where they planned to live with Amrita's parents. She would continue to paint and he was to set up his practice there. Unfortunately, things didn't go as planned, for Marie Antoinette made it as difficult as possible for the young couple to settle down. Marie would speak insultingly to Victor, often when Amrita was not present.

Despite the tension at home, Amrita managed to make a painting of four women and a young girl with a basket of flowers, surrounded by foliage. The situation at home was resolved when Amrita's cousin Kirpal Singh Majithia invited her and Victor to live with him in Saraya. Once they arrived at Saraya, however, at the house known as the Big Kothi, life was still tough. Victor had no work and Amrita found that the lack of stimulating atmosphere made her spirits sag. The couple had only one room to themselves, and the family, however likeable, seemed a constant overbearing presence, an encroachment on their privacy.

Marie Antoinette's resentment towards Victor would haunt Amrita's marriage for the rest of her life. While Victor maintained a civil demeanour towards her, she libelled him both openly, to his face and behind his back, to Amrita and Umrao Singh. Finally he wrote to her, hoping to bridge the ever widening gap between them, his language indicating their distance. He addressed Marie Antoinette in the third person. In a letter written on 13 April 1940 from Saraya, he pleaded:

"Dear Mici Nene

I have decided so many times to write to you but pessimistic feelings would overcome me and I would give up. A few times I was on the verge of writing but Mici Nene wrote a few disappointing letters to me humiliating me with comments about what

I should do or not do, knocking out my will to write. About this situation I wrote to Umrao Uncle but now I want to write to you. Inspite of Mici Nene's behaviour, I don't feel any kind of anger because I can understand everything. Amri and I discussed how we can put an end to this situation and we realised that it is only possible if we can make Mici Nene understand that we are not enemies and we really do have the best feelings towards her. I don't feel angry, just a disappointment...please believe me that later on all of us will think about the past not as a cruel time but as a time of mistakes. I am kissing your hands with the wish that everything will be fine and we will lead our lives in the future peacefully."

(Above letter is in the possession of the family members.)

Things, however, did not take a turn for the better and they continued to get accusing and vilifying letters from Marie Antoinette. The chasm between Amrita's parents and the young couple seemed unbridgeable, to the point where there was no question of retracing their steps. The uncertainty of their future in Saraya hung over them like a cloud. That unsettled state of affairs was not a good beginning for a marriage. Though Amrita continued to paint, her depression lingered. Gradually, her spirits revived and she got back to work and life at Saraya began to feel more settled. She wrote to her parents on 14 August 1940...

"*We are so pleased and happy: and though the work is tremendously fatiguing and there is so much of it that Victor comes home in the evening with his head reeling, utterly exhausted. Yet both he and I are happy at our being, at last independent that he does not mind it at all and works overtime with great enthusiasm. I too am producing good things. The only thing to make our happiness complete would be to have a little home. The question has not yet been decided and at present we are still staying with the family, which just now is not unpleasant as they are away but tends to become rather burdensome when they are all here. But still all that to us at present is vastly compensated by the fact that Victor has got a job and not such a bad one either, far better than we hoped for in fact and we are quite satisfied with our lot.*"

(The above letter mentioned in Sundaram, Kapur, Sheikh, Subramanyan, *Amrita Shergil*)

Amrita's emotions were going through a roller coaster ride. August she seemed fine but by November her spirits started to sink again. Part of the problem seemed to have been her continually cramped existence. Victor's salary as a doctor at the sugar factory was the princely sum of Rs.160, a pittance even in those days. Amrita received an additional Rs. 100 from her family, but that did not meet their basic requirements. She wrote to her mother how it was physically impossible to manage on that sum of money when they lacked the basic things needed in a household, like cooking utensils, dishes, tea set and curtains. She also felt they needed a car as for Victor time was precious and they couldn't possibly go on using the family's car forever. (Mentioned in Iqbal Singh's book – *Amrita Shergil*)

Amrita was beginning to lose her zest for life. She was hardly the happy person with rich, full life, radiating joy where ever she went. She was fast losing all her flexibility, her interest in people and the desire to approach them. She felt grey and unbelievably empty. That bleakness had begun to infect her marriage. "*I and Victor are tremendously fond of each other. When we are alone together, we sit by the hour in silence, he begins to yawn, and I sink deeper and deeper into a depressed and depressing silence and we weigh intolerably on each other till unable to bear it longer one of us gets up and suggests a game of patience or chess. All this seems very depressing and at moments it does get me down, just as it gets down Victor (though of course neither of us utters a word about it), but when I come to analyse it, it ceases to depress me. Between people of sensibility who are placed too close together, there sometimes develops a barrier apparently insurmountable, of self-consciousness, a sort of moral cramp, an inability to approach*" (mentioned in Sundaram, Kapur, Sheikh, Subramanyan, *Amrita Shergil*)

By July, Amrita's depression had further deepened. In early June, both Victor and Amrita had gone to Lahore on an exploratory visit to see if they could relocate themselves there. They returned, with Amrita spending a brief while in Simla while Victor resumed his work in Saraya, with the tentative affirmation of their desire to leave for Lahore. July 1941 – Amrita wrote, "*I haven't touched a brush or gone near a canvas for four months. I don't know why. I am gripped by a sort of fear whenever I think of working again. I suppose one can get out of the habit of painting.*"

A change of location was, Amrita rightly surmised, a possible way out of the cul-de-sac they had both reached. The time had come to leave Saraya, and since Simla was untenable, Amrita and Victor finally decided in favour of Lahore.

5. NEHRU AND KHUSHWANT EPISODES

Amrita's exhibition was held with those of the Ukil brothers and some of their students at the Imperial Hotel on 27 February 1937, inaugurated by the Raja of Phaltan. Nehru attended and Amrita described their meeting in a letter from Simla,

"I think he liked me too, as much as I liked him. He came to my exhibition and we had a long chat. He wrote to me some time back (after he had met me at the exhibition): 'I like your pictures because they showed so much strength and perception. You have both these qualities. How different these paintings were from the pasty-faced lifeless efforts that one sees so frequently in India!!'" (Letter dated 17 April 1937, Ibid)

Amrita met Nehru once or twice after that but they seemed to have exchanged letters quite actively. The exact nature of their relationship is difficult to gauge, because many of Nehru's letters were later burnt by Amrita's parents, much to her disappointment, while she was away in Budapest getting married. Their explanation for that was that they were clearing her things and thought she had left the letters behind because she did not need them. Amrita wrote to them in summer of 1938 with a sense of hurt, "*I must admit that it was a bit of a shock to hear that all my letters are being perused and consigned to flames! I had already made a spring cleaning among them and burnt and destroyed a whole room full of letters some weeks before my departure. Those letters I had specifically kept, either because they were dear to me, amused me or were important from an artistic point of view or otherwise. However, it is no use crying over spilt milk. I merely hope that atleast the letters of Marie, Karl and Jawahar Lal Nehru have been spared. I had left them behind not because I thought them dangerous witnesses of my past but because I didn't wish to increase my already heavy luggage... However, now I suppose I have to resign myself to a bleak old age unrelieved by the entertainment that the perusal of old love letters would have afforded it.*" *(*Mentioned in Sundaram, Kapur, Sheikh, Subramanyan, *Amrita Shergil)*

Yet one letter from Amrita to Nehru, written on 6 November 1937, which remained in his collection provides not only a glimmer of their relationship but also Amrita's own ability to see people shorn of their mystique and to be able to relate to them in the forthright manner. It also reveals how a man much older than herself and of national eminence could be drawn to not just her attractive demeanour but her charismatic aura:

"A little while ago somebody said to me 'You know Jawahar Lal Nehru is ill'. I hadn't known it. I never read the papers. I have been thinking of you a great deal but somehow, perhaps for that very reason, I hadn't felt like writing. Your letter came as a surprise. I need hardly add an extremely pleasant one. Thanks for the book. As a rule I dislike biographies and autobiographies. They ring false. Pomposity or exhibitionism. But I think I'll like yours. You are able to discard your halo occasionally. You are capable of saying 'When I saw the sea for the first time' when others would say 'When the sea saw me for the first time'. I should have liked to have known you better. I am always attracted to people who are integral enough to be inconsistent without discordance and who don't trail viscous threads of regrets behind them. I don't think that it is on the threshold of life that one feels chaotic, it is when one has crossed the threshold that one discovers that things which looked simple are definitely torturous and complex. That it is only in inconsistency that there is any consistency. But of course you have an orderly mind.

I don't think you were interested in my paintings really. You looked at my pictures without seeing them.

You are not hard. You have got a mellow face. I like your face. It is sensual, sensitive and detached at the same time. I am enclosing a cutting that my father asked me to forward to you. It was written by him."

(As mentioned in Jawahar Lal Nehru, *A Bunch of Old Letters,* Penguin Books India, New Delhi – 2004)

The above distinctly personal note seemed to have arisen from an earlier correspondence that is no longer traceable. Many questions remain unanswered. Why did she not paint his portrait? Iqbal Singh, whom she met in Simla in 1937 and who became a close friend and confidant, seemed to have asked her, and she replied that she would never paint Nehru because "he is too good looking." Just like everyone else, I wonder, did she have an affair with him? If so, was it a serious affair or mild flirtation? Victor Egan's daughters from his second marriage seem to have been sure that she did not have an affair with Nehru because she was already in love with Victor. Somewhere in the hazy sheaves of her consciousness were these questions answered or did they remain unknown even to her own self?

THE KHUSHWANT EPISODE

Khushwant met Amrita just twice but those meetings remained etched in his memory. One summer, her last one, Khushwant heard that she and her Hungarian cousin husband had taken an apartment across the road to where he lived in Lahore. He was meant to set up his medical practice and she, her painting studio. She had a large number of friends and admirers in the city and also had rich, land-owning relatives on her father's side who regularly visited Lahore.

One afternoon, Khushwant came home to find his flat full of aroma of expensive French perfume. He tiptoed to the kitchen and asked his cook about the visitor. "A Memsahib in a sari," he informed him. The cook had told the lady that his Sahib would be home for lunch any moment. She had helped herself to a bottle of beer from the fridge. Khushwant was sure somehow that his uninvited guest could be no other than Amrita Shergil.

Amrita enjoyed drawing men towards her like iron filings to a magnet. As she entered the room, Khushwant stood up to greet her. "You must be Amrita Shergil," he said. She nodded. Without apologising for helping herself to his beer she proceeded to tell him as to why she had come to see him. All mundane matters – she wanted to know about plumbers, dhobis, carpenters, cooks, etc. she could hire in the neighbourhood. After she finished talking, she looked around the room. He pointed to a few paintings hanging there and said, "These are by my wife. She's an amateur." Amrita glanced at them and scoffed, "That is obvious." Khushwant was taken aback by her disdain and did not know how to retort.

Khuswant's wife along with their seven-month-old son had gone to their home 'Sunderban' in Mashobra, seven miles beyond Simla. A few weeks later he joined his family there. Amrita at that time was staying with Chaman Lals who had rented a house above Khushwant's father's. An invitation for lunch was extended. The three of them – Chaman, his wife Helen and Amrita came at midday. Seven months old Rahul was in the playpen teaching himself how to stand on his feet. Every one took turns to compliment Khushwant's wife for producing such an adorable baby. When everybody had finished, Amrita gave the child a long look and remarked, "What an ugly little boy!" Everyone froze. Some protested against those unkind words and Khushwant's wife said to him very firmly, "I am not having that lady in my house again." Amrita got to know about it and told people, "I will teach that woman a lesson she won't forget. I will seduce her husband."

But that never happened because they never met again…

6. SHADES OF LIFE

Amrita came over to Simla from Lahore only to find that her sister Indira and her husband had occupied her studio. She shifted to another part of the house but had no place to paint. After a few days, she had a major flare up with Indira. According to Iqbal Singh, (in his book about Amrita) Amrita was very fond of Indu but there was always an undercurrent of jealousy on Indu's part. Victor felt that had to do with Amrita's beauty and social success. Because of her great intelligence and social charm, Amrita attracted people much more and was always more in demand, which Indu resented. When Amrita and Victor first arrived in India after their marriage, Indu and her husband Kalyan were very well off while the former had nothing. Indu showed off on that account and that increased the distance between the two.

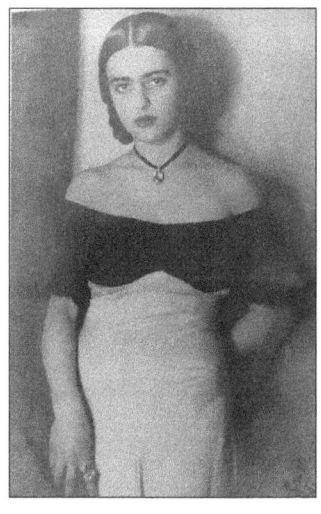

One night, according to Iqbal Singh's account, Indira held a dinner party at which the chief guests were three foreign men. Upon seeing Amrita's paintings on the walls, they took a great interest in her and talked mainly to her over dinner, about herself and her work. Amrita could sense that Indu was very upset and tried to draw her into the conversation, but they were mainly interested in her. After dinner they wanted to see her studio, were most impressed by her paintings and continued talking to her for the rest of the evening. Iqbal Singh specifically mentioned that after they left, Indu ranted and raved, angrily accusing Amrita of constantly trying to steal the limelight. Finally Amrita said, "Well, if that's the way you feel about me, I think I had better leave, and not be under your roof any longer." Indu screamed, "Yes, go... Go away." Without packing a single bag, Amrita left and walked to Helen's house, arriving at three in the morning, having walked over ten miles uphill. Surprised Helen took her under her wings in no time.

Reading and researching about Amrita Shergil, collecting the blissful and gloomy moments of her life, I am compelled to think and rethink about the complexities of human thought process and actions and the inevitable arbitrariness of judging another's behaviour. From a distance, everybody's life entices and has that 'wow' factor... It's only when we step into their shoes do we realise that they too have had their fair share of lows and blues and they were as human and as mortal as any of us.

Amrita had complicated relations with her mother and her sister back home but Victor was her umbrella in that rough weather. Finally in Lahore, they had a place they could call their own – a rented apartment 23 in Sir Ganga Ram Mansion, also known as Exchange Mansion, which was occupied mostly by professionals. Victor had his clinic on the ground floor, the living rooms on the first floor and the *barsati* on top was Amrita's studio. Visitors often caught Amrita and Victor in dungarees, polishing the doors, painting the doors and windows.

Lahore then became the hub of art for a few years. The city's artist community included Abdul Rehman Chugtai, Bevan Petman (Amrita's childhood drawing teacher) and Satish Gujral. Khushwant Singh held a fortnightly soiree at his residence with writers and poets like Faiz Ahmed Faiz, Ahmed Shah Bokhari, Gurbax Singh, Kartar Singh Duggal, Amrita Pritam, GD Khosla and many others.

In the midst of that effervescent atmosphere, Amrita strove to express her own creativity. By October she felt quite settled in her flat and wrote to her mother, *"I have got this little extra room ready for Duci. I am not sure the cook would produce Indian food to his liking but I know Duci is not particularly fussy. I do wish he would make up his mind to come here soon."*

By that time, Amrita had decided to have an exhibition in December. The show was to be held at the Punjab Literary League, above Lorang's Swiss Café in the Charing Cross area, and in all likelihood it was partly sponsored by the League whose president

Sir Abdul Qadir was an old family friend. Amrita asked her friend Karl Khandalavala to write an introduction for the catalogue, saying that if he didn't have time, she would use one he had written earlier. She wrote that she considered Karl the only one competent to 'judge and evaluate' her work and expressed her keenness to have the introduction by him. (As mentioned in Iqbal Singh's, *Amrita Shergil,* page 167). She also invited Bokhari to write in her catalogue. Eventually, her paintings arrived from Simla and she went with Victor to personally inspect the exhibition hall.

Amrita was excited about the exhibition. She had begun work on what she did not realise would be her last painting. She painted the view from her apartment which consisted of mud houses and buffaloes kept by the milk man who lived there. The painting had four buffaloes; two squatting in the front, one near the trough and another with a crow perched on its snout. A woman in red veil bending over cow dung cakes can be viewed on the roof. A vivid painting in burnt earth tones. The painting was never completed but in casting aside the last remnants of Amrita's inheritance and past training to achieve a new freedom of space and form, it speaks of the boundless horizons that were beginning to open for her. The veteran artist K. G. Subramanyan elucidated: "*The last painting she has left us, seems to be one in which she definitely did not feel oppressed by either the Indian scene or the Indian manner and had found her freedom, while retaining at the same time 'contact with the soil' for she so passionately yearned.*"

7. AND SHE SLIPPED OUT OF THE HANDS OF LIFE

Amrita had barely two weeks left before her mid-December exhibition when she took ill. Iqbal Singh, who visited her every day, discovered her sickness by accident. He used to meet her almost every day after work at a sort of salon where she entertained her friends and admirers. For some reason it so happened that he didn't see her for a couple of days. On 3rd December, he went to her house and found it unusually quiet. Victor wasn't in his clinic, so he went up and knocked at her bedroom door. On entering he saw Amrita lying in bed, looking extremely pale. She said she had eaten some *pakoras* at Sir Abdul and Lady Qadir's house about three days back and was suffering from acute dysentery ever since. She said Victor had given her medicines and she would be well soon. Iqbal Singh chatted with her for a while and left, assuming the condition was temporary. On the evening of 5th December, he arrived at their apartment and found Victor descending the stairs, looking grim. On being asked what the matter was he replied that Amrita was gravely ill and that she probably won't survive. She was in coma and he was doing his best to save her. Iqbal Singh drove to Helen's house and returned with Helen and her husband. (As mentioned in Iqbal Singh's book, *Amrita Shergil*, page 169-70)

Helen rushed to Amrita's room. She came out and reported that Amrita was really dying and both of them went to get another doctor. Dr. Nihal Chand Sikri and the German doctor Dr. Kalisch examined her and said it was too late as peritonitis had set in and her intestines had perforated which would result in her bleeding to death.

It seems that Amrita's nephew Charanjit Singh Mann, who happened to be present, was later asked by Victor to fetch Dr. Raghubir Singh, another well-known physician from Lahore. By the time he reached to examine Amrita, she had passed away. Charanjit recalled: "*I had driven up from Gujranwala which was about an hour away and dropped in on them, Victor came down the stairs looking very depressed and said – She is not well. So I gave up the idea of the hockey match and decided to stay with them because as a family member I may be of some help. The third night I told Victor to call another doctor. But he said – I know what I am doing. Later when the doctor came, he said it was too late.*" (Charanjit Singh Mann said this in an interview with Yashodhara Dalmi in New Delhi, January 2002)

Around midnight Amrita passed away. She was only twenty eight. The news shook everyone as they gathered in her apartment the next day. Her parents drove up from Simla, Indira and Kalyan from New Delhi. Umrao Singh poignantly noted in his recollections, "*I could not fully believe that Amrita was dead. Without tears and sobs, in a dazed condition, we reached Lahore about six in the evening. We rushed upstairs and entered the bedroom, saw her covered with a shawl. Uncovering her face, we found her dead and cold... Next morning Amrita's body was taken to the crematory. Those fingers which had painted and that brain which had conceived her works, receiving its inspiration from the deathless spirit, were dissolving into the elements in front of our eyes...she*

had entered the prenatal world at Lahore and death seemed to have conspired with life, to release her spirit from its physical chrysalis in the same city..."
(From Umrao Singh Shergil's 'Some Reminiscences of Amrita Shergil' Usha, Amrita Shergil special)

The family decided to cremate Amrita's body and hold a Sikh funeral. This took place the next day, Sunday, 7th December, with her body covered by a Kashmiri shawl. At the last moment it was found that no flowers had been laid on her. So friends with gardens rushed to bring some back. The cortege, accompanied by around thirty to forty mourners, moved through the Mall and Lower Mall, past the Badshahi Mosque and the Lahore fort, and finally to the burning ghats on the river Ravi. Umrao Singh lit the funeral pyre after a brief religious ceremony. And as the flames consumed her body, everyone present there had the feeling that there would never be any one like her ever again...

8. AFTER SHE LEFT

Amrita's sudden death left both her family and Lahore's artistic community stunned. A condolence meet was held at the Punjab Literary League, which was attended by Chughtai, Sanyal, Roop and Mary Krishna and many other friends. Letters of condolence started pouring in from far and wide. One of the most poignant one was from Jawahar Lal Nehru from Anand Bhavan, Allahabad to Amrita's mother, Marie Antoinette-

"My dear Mrs. Shergil,

During the past five years or so, I met Amrita about half a dozen times only, after long intervals. But the very first time I met her I was much struck by her genius and her charm. I was greatly attracted to her and we became friends. I felt that she was very precious to India and I looked forward to the ripening of her genius. I had hoped that she would be able to come to Allahabad and spend a few days with us and she had almost promised to do so.

These memories are of past now. I cannot tell you how shocked and pained I was to learn of her sudden death. The bright flower of her sudden life, from which so much was expected, suddenly wilting away and falling was a great blow. Often I thought of her. If I felt the blow so much, I can well imagine what you and her father felt. It is rather futile my expressing sympathy, for that is almost meaningless. But I do assure you that your great sorrow was shared by a large number of people who had the privilege to come in contact with Amrita. I shall treasure her memory.

I am sending you back the various magazines and papers you sent me. Only one thing I have taken out and kept...Amrita's photograph." (As mentioned in *Usha*, Amrita Sher Gil special issue, Lahore, August 1942, page-5)

Another touching letter came from Sarojini Naidu, written from Hyderabad to the parents on 10 December 1941 – "*Had she lived she would have been among the greatest artists modern India has produced; as it is, the work she has left is a legacy of which her country should be proud. Such vigour, such daring, such originality and she nothing more than a child in years. Please accept my affection for her as my message of sympathy and sorrow in your loss which is also a loss to the great world of Art.*"

Did Amrita have a premonition that she was going to die? To sketch a funeral procession and express a desire to paint it does seem to indicate, if not conscious knowledge, certainly an intuition of her forthcoming death. Victor seems to have thought so, too. He mentioned that Amrita often had the feeling that she would die very young. Though there were no physical symptoms, she just felt that her life would be short. She often used to tell Victor, "I have to work hard, I have to work fast, because my time is very short." And that she had to hurry because she hadn't much time left. (As told by Victor Egan, in Iqbal Singh's Amrita Sher Gil, Page-182)

Not long after Amrita left, her mother grew hysterical with rage and sent all her acquaintances volcanic letters accusing Victor of killing her daughter in cold blood. Amrita's father, on the other hand, maintained a dignified silence. Nothing was clear and evident about the cause of Amrita's death. Letters exchanged between Victor and Umrao Singh indicate that she ate *pakoras* at a tea party at the home of her parent's friend Sir Abdul Qadir, and that gave her bacillary dysentery. Her friend Iqbal believed that she wouldn't lie about anything and if she had said that she felt sick after having the *pakoras*, it had to be the truth.

In contrast, Khushwant Singh, who was based in Lahore at that time recalled, "*It took some time for Amrita's mother to get the details of her daughter's illness and death. She held her nephew and son-in-law responsible. Murder, I am certain, it was not. Carelessness, I am certain, it was. My version of death came from Dr. Raghubir Singh. He was summoned to Amrita's bedside at midnight when she was beyond hope of recovery. He believed that she had become pregnant with Victor's child and had been aborted by her husband. The operation had gone wrong. She had bled profusely and developed peritonitis. Her husband wanted Dr. Raghubir to give her blood transfusion and offered his own blood for it. Dr. Raghubir refused to do without finding the blood groupings. While the two doctors were arguing with each other, Amrita slipped out of life.*" (From Khushwant Singh's book – Truth, Love and a Little Malice... Page 98-99)

At any rate, Amrita's death hung like a shadow over Victor and caused immense turmoil at many levels. It was, of course, her mother who cried the loudest and considered herself the most deeply devastated, yet she turned to Victor for help when her mental health began to deteriorate. Increasingly, Marie turned to Victor and gave graphic accounts of her illness but it is not clear whether she did anything to help herself. Towards the end of her life, she seemed to have crossed the line of any remedy. Finally, she shot herself with Umrao Singh's gun in his study on 31 July 1948. Umrao Singh went to live with Indira in Simla and in Delhi until he died in 1954, at the age of 84. He eventually lost his memory in his last days and once or twice, it is said, he wandered away for hours, leaving Indu and her husband frantic. Indira was to pass prematurely in 1974 in Kasauli, where she lived by herself for many years, leaving behind her two children Vivan and Navina. In December 1954, almost 13 years after Amrita's death, Victor married Nina Hydrie. Their daughter, Eva remembers her childhood and youth with nostalgia. She said, *"Time passed joyfully, although in an unstated manner there was always the presence of Amrita. I grew up with Amrita in the background. She was neither an over romanticised nor ominous presence. She quite simply marked a phase in Dad's life. Had it not been for her, Dad might never have left Europe. Had it not been for her, I might never have been!!!"*

Victor passed away in June 1997, at the age of 86. He had had a bad fall and was permanently bedridden. He developed bed sores that turned septic no matter what the family did to help. It was so bad that he contemplated euthanasia. The Majithia family saw to it that he was cremated according to the Sikh rites. Victor had always wanted to be cremated but he wanted no gravestones, no markers and no memories.

9. IN MEMORY OF AMRITA

In the context of talking about Amrita's contribution to Indian art, it is imperative that each one of us attends to the question of preservation and restoration of her paintings. Neither her family nor the Government of India has initiated a museum devoted to her work. Of her 143 listed paintings, most remain with relatives, some of the choice ones with Indira's children. All 45 of her works that were with Victor – barring only his own portrait were donated to the National Gallery of Modern Art in New Delhi. Many of her works with Umrao Singh were also donated to the museum. Together they form an important component of the museum's collection and are displayed in the special section of the building.

The government's acquisition of the paintings however, was not without its drawbacks. Many of her paintings there seem to have suffered from mishandling. *The Statesman* of 30 July 1959 reported that Indira had written to the Prime Minister Nehru about a year earlier, saying that the paintings had got a raw deal from the government. Initially, they had been stowed in the attic of the secretariat and deteriorated. When they came to the museum, Indira alleged, more than three quarters of them were locked away in a small ante room, the handsome frames were replaced by plain, unattractive ones and some of the captions were changed. "It breaks my heart," she wrote, "to see the shabby and negligent manner in which my sister's great legacy to the country is being treated by unappreciative people. If my sister's paintings cannot be exhibited in the National Gallery in an adequate manner, for lack of space or any other reason, I would gladly receive back a number of them and hang them up where they deserve to be." The Prime Minister's principal private secretary replied that he was glad that his attention had been drawn to the matter and he would write to the concerned Ministry to find out why this had happened.

In his defence, the curator of the museum responded that Amrita's paintings formed the nucleus of The National Gallery of Modern Art when it was founded in 1954, and since 1956 they had all been placed in air conditioned rooms. Some were in bad condition so they were being restored by a German conservationist.

Embalmed forever in the stately halls of the National Gallery, Amrita's paintings remind us of her passionate quest for an authenticity of means and expression in art. Her works are generally never sold in the market: on the rare occasions when they are, they fetch unbelievably high prices. How ironic that not even a portion of that wealth was accessible to the artist in her lifetime, and she had to run from pillar to post for a few hundred rupees. She could not have known that after her death, her life and work would become something of a legend. Yet even if she had, she would have lived and struggled in the same way, and made the most of her short, productive and unforgettable life…

QUOTES ABOUT AMRITA AND HER WORK

"I have always been a fan of Salvador Dali, but Amrita Shergil, who was an Indian-Hungarian painter, is another favourite. She was painting Indian women, and growing up here, I'd never seen anyone paint Indian women, so that was really incredible to see a painting of someone who looks like you. I think that has a lot of impact on you."

– Rupi Kaur, Canadian Poetess of Indian origin

"Amrita is unique in her own way – unique in her colour palette, which is far different than being western and is international in every sense. It's the epitome of Indian sensuality and passion. She's a master artist above all. That's our Amrita."

– Anamika Bandopadhyay, Film maker